Rhetoric & Prosody

(A handbook of Figures of Speech, rhymes, feet of poetic lines for High School Students)

Mr. Peter

Made with ❤ on the Notion Press Platform

www.notionpress.com

DEDICATION

Dedicated to my elder child who came to me with his questions to know of simile, metaphor, and on another day with alliteration, personification and rhyme.

Writer's Academic works:
1. Study of Nouns, Pronouns, Adjectives & Articles (detail study) ISBN: 979-842-211-856-4 / 979-888-704-109-4
2. All about Verbs (Forms, Functions, Conjugation, Tense, Voice Change, Forming Questions & Negation)   ISBN: 979-840-441-149-2 / 979-888-704-411-8
3. Study of Adverbs, Prepositions, Conjunctions & Interjections ISBN: 979-840-785-010-6 / 979-888-704-532-0
4. Detail Study of Phrases, Clauses & Sentences, including Idioms & Phrasal Verbs ISBN: 979-840-881-405-3 / 979-888-704-582-5
5. Study of Subject-Verb Agreement, Narration Change, Use of Punctuation; including Analysis, Synthesis & Split-up (Study through charts, division, explanation and examples) ISBN: 979-880-723-013-3 / 979-888-704-674-7
6. **Peter's 'English Grammar, A Complete Version of English Grammar,** (detail study, explanation & examples) ISBN: 979-879-725-020-3 / 979-888-704-463-7
7. **Question Bank of English Grammar & Composition (Learn through Exercises)** ISBN: 979-883-531-890-2 / 979-888-733-132-4
8. **Rhetoric & Prosody** (A handbook of Figures of Speech, rhymes, feet of poetic lines for High School Students) ISBN: 979-840-526-645-9 / 979-888-684-952-3
9. Picture Composition; For Primary Level, Std-I to V (Development of Writing Skill from Single Sentence Formation to Paragraph Writing, incl. question patterns and answer guide) ISBN: 979-888-805-249-5 (B&W) / 979-888-783-066-7 (color print)
10. Steps to Composition (Development of Writing Skill, Part-1), includes Picture Composition, Essay & Story Writing ISBN: 979-884-408-069-2 / 979-888-805-001-9
11. Development of Writing Skill, Part-2 (includes Letter Writing- Business Letters, Application for Jobs, Letters to Editor, bank authorities, Institutional Heads & others) ISBN: 979-835-689-886-0 / 979-888-833-455-3
12. Development of Writing Skill, Part-3 (includes- E-mails, Poster Making, Notices, Processing, Dialogue, Article, Speech & Debate Writing as well as Diary entry, Summary and Reporting) ISBN: 979-836-392-249-7 / 979-888-869-544-9
13. **A Book of Advanced Writing Skill, the Complete Version** (incl Part-1, 2 & 3) ISBN: 979-836-472-826-5 / 979-888-869-835-8

Author page URL's:

https://www.amazon.com/author/mr.peter

https://www.amazon.in/~/e/B09QW2P4TY *(For Indians, this and next)*

https://notionpress.com/store/s?NP_Books%5Bquery%5D=Mr.+Peter

https://www.amazon.co.uk/~/e/B09QW2P4TY

https://www.amazon.de/~/e/B09QW2P4TY

https://www.amazon.fr/~/e/B09QW2P4TY

https://www.amazon.co.jp/~/e/B09QW2P4TY

https://www.amazon.es/~/e/B09QW2P4TY

https://www.amazon.it/~/e/B09QW2P4TY

https://www.amazon.com.br/kindle-dbs/entity/author?asin=B09QW2P4TY

For Readers from India and nearby, you may place order with **notionpress.com**
Visit **notionpress.com** and type 'Mr. Peter' in the search box; give order of books to **avail elegant discounts** *using the following* **Coupon Codes;** as, unique00, bulk00, Deal1 and so on against the books: (if not work, contact to https://www.facebook.com/profile.php?id=100081822070172 or (5) Books Campaigns, Free Coupons, Learning English Grammar & Composition | Facebook

Coupon Codes	Book Name	Buy for	Discount %	Rebate Prices
unique00	**Advanced Writing Skill, the Complete Version** (incl. Part-1, 2 & 3)	1 copy	15	~~780~~ 663
PujaDeal10	Development of Writing Skill, Part-3	1 copy	18	~~365~~ 300
PujaDeal9	Development of Writing Skill, Part-2	1 copy	18	~~365~~ 300
PujaDeal8	Steps to Composition (Development of Writing Skill, Part-1)	1 copy	20	~~300~~ 240
PujaDeal7	**Rhetoric & Prosody**	1 copy	20	~~240~~ 192

PujaDeal6	**Question Bank of English Grammar & Composition**	1 copy	20	~~559~~ 448	
PujaDeal5	Study of Subject-Verb Agreement, Narration Change, Use of Punctuation; including Analysis, Synthesis & Split-up	1 copy	20	~~301~~ 241	
PujaDeal4	Detail Study of Phrases, Clauses & Sentences, including Idioms & Phrasal Verbs	1 copy	20	~~290~~ 232	
PujaDeal3	Study of Adverbs, Prepositions, Conjunctions & Interjections	1 copy	20	~~260~~ 208	
PujaDeal2	All about Verbs (Forms, Functions, Conjugation, Tense, Voice Change, Forming Questions & Negation)	1 copy	18	~~420~~ 345	
PujaDeal1	Study of Nouns, Pronouns, Adjectives & Articles (detail study)	1 copy	20	~~280~~ 224	
unique01	**Peter's 'English Grammar'** (Complete Version of English Grammar)	1 copy	23	~~1201~~ 925	
FOR COPIES MORE THAN ONE					
bulk00	**Advanced Writing Skill, the Complete Version** (incl. Part-1, 2 & 3)	2 to 5000 copies	23	~~780~~ 601	
Deal11	Development of Writing Skill, Part-3	2 to 5000 copies	24	~~365~~ 278	
Deal10	Development of Writing Skill, Part-2	2 to 5000 copies	24	~~365~~ 278	
Deal9	Steps to Composition (Development of Writing Skill, from Primary to Secondary Level)	2 to 5000 copies	26	~~300~~ 222	
Deal8	**Rhetoric & Prosody**	2 to 5000 copies	26	~~240~~ 178	
Deal7	**Question Bank of English Grammar & Composition**	2 to 5000 copies	28	~~559~~ 403	
bulk01	**Peter's 'English Grammar'** (Complete Version of English Grammar)	2 to 5000 copies	30	~~1201~~ 841	
Deal5	Study of Subject-Verb Agreement, Narration Change, Use of Punctuation; including Analysis, Synthesis & Split-up	2 to 5000 copies	26	~~301~~ 223	
Deal4	Detail Study of Phrases, Clauses & Sentences, including Idioms & Phrasal Verbs	2 to 5000 copies	26	~~290~~ 215	
Deal3	Study of Adverbs, Prepositions, Conjunctions & Interjections	2 to 5000 copies	26	~~260~~ 193	
Deal2	All about Verbs (Forms, Functions, Conjugation, Tense, Voice Change, Forming Questions & Negation)	2 to 5000 copies	26	~~420~~ 311	
Deal1	Study of Nouns, Pronouns, Adjectives & Articles (detail study)	2 to 5000 copies	26	~~280~~ 208	

CONTENTS

ACKNOWLEDGMENTS

Peter pays tribute for his book 'Rhetoric & Prosody' to 'The Anatomy of Rhetoric & Prosody' by Gopal Mallik Thakur.

Outline of the Book

The book 'Rhetoric & Prosody, a handbook of Figures of Speech, rhymes, feet of poetic lines for High School Students' is purely designed for high school students. The book includes chapters covering **Rhetoric, the seven class of Figures of Speech** which are termed often as ornamentation of our daily speech or the speech of a leader, writer, etc., to impress their customers, audience or listeners. The book includes simile, metaphor, antithesis, epigram, oxymoron, metonymy, synecdoche, hypallage, personification, pathetic fallacy, apostrophe, vision, hyperbole, irony, euphemism, alliteration, pun, and many others along with short discussion and examples against each of them; **and in the section of Prosody (the Grammar of Verse)** the book includes rhyme, meter, foot of a poetic line and the art of scansion for proper understanding of poetic lines and to know its rhyme (also 'Rime') and meter, besides introduction as well of some verse forms and literary terms, definitions and examples, as far it was possible for Peter.

The book contains an illustrated table of contents, not to give his readers the impression what his book contains or has, but always for your help, so that you can jump to any point (figures of your choice and need) and save your invaluable time.

Finally, if you feel, it made you help to get understand the topics discussed, the writer likes to pay gratitude and give you lot of thanks; if not, he seeks forgiveness for your time and fruitless attempt.

Section-A. Rhetoric (Figures of Speech)

We have already learnt of **'Parts of Speech'** that builds a statement, question, order, etc. by proper sequence or arrangement of words. **'Rhetoric & Prosody'** do the function of ornamentation of that speech, i.e., statement, question, and order, to make them impressive — is termed as the **rhetoric figures of speech.**
The word **'rhetoric'** comes from Greek word **'rhetor',** meaning 'a public speaker'. In ancient Greece & Rome 'oratory' was a part of rhetoric, the art of speaking before the public in a persuasive manner. Simply, it is the **'art of speech'**, *used to persuade, convince, move or impress the listener.* Pause or rhythm, and tone—are important with the arrangement of words, not like in parts of speech, but slightly in a different look and presentation. Later it was broadly received in literature (*i.e., began to use in prose, poetry, verse & widely popularized in drama in order to move the feelings of readers or audience, or so-called spectators effectively*).

Grammar, Rhetoric & Prosody: Both **'grammar'** and **'rhetoric'**- are concerned with the rules of composition & order of words in a sentence. However, their aims are different. While **grammar** aims at correctness of expression, **Rhetoric**, in addition to this, aims at making the expression beautiful and forceful. Actually, where grammar ends, rhetoric begins (*but of course not like that rhetoric begins at the end of a sentence*). The process goes on simultaneously, following the rules of grammar and considering the aim to make the expression more beautiful, expressive and forceful than by an ordinary statement or question. Both composition and beautification go along in rhetoric, and thus, rhetoric has no contradiction with the grammar.

On the other hand, **'prosody'** is called the 'Grammar of Verse'. It looks after and takes special care for rhythm of a verse (a poetic line or two), so that it sounds musical, touch heart of the listeners.

The 7 Class of Figures of Speech

❏ Our thoughts and ideas can be expressed plainly or elegantly. The study of grammar of language teaches us to express our ideas properly and correctly. Rhetoric teaches us to express those ideas or thoughts more gracefully, elegantly or influentially what we intend to say or deliver.

For memorable and effective expression, we must use the **'figures of speech',** *popularly known as* **rhetoric.** So, the figures are the means wherewith we embellish our style of speaking expressive and beautiful. Study the class of Figures.

The figures can be grouped into 7 classes:
1. Figures based on Similarity,
2. Figures based on Difference,
3. Figures based on Association,
4. Figures based on Imagination,
5. Figures based on Indirectness,
6. Figures based on Sound,
7. Figures based on Construction.

We intended to choose only the selected ones from each class as far we can for the high school students, and for the same we have taken special care for simple illustrations with examples for each of them which are chosen for discussion.

Where an advanced learner needs or feels for more information, explanation, examples, they may take help of a book, better than this one and highly enriched with.

✶ However, we have chosen the followings ones for our discussion, illustration and to realize them through examples, which are following after each illustration:

Rhetoric Group or Class	*Figures of Speech*
1. 'Figures based on Similarity'	1) *Simile,* 2) *Metaphor,* 3) *Allegory,* 4) *Parable* & 5) *Fable;*
2. 'Figures based on Difference'	6) *Antithesis,* 7) *Epigram,* 8) *Paradox,* 9) *Oxymoron,* 10) *Climax,* 11) *Anticlimax;*
3. 'Figures based on Association'	12) *Metonymy,* 13) *Synecdoche,* 14) *Hypallage (Transferred Epithet),* 15) *Allusion;*

4. 'Figures based on Imagination'	16) *Personification*, 17) *Personal Metaphor*, 18) *Apostrophe*, 19) *Pathetic Fallacy*, 20) *Vision*, 21) *Hyperbole (Exaggeration)*;
5. 'Figures based on Indirectness'	22) *Innuendo*, 23) *Irony*, 24) *Sarcasm*, 25) *Periphrasis*, 26) *Euphemism*, 27) *Meiosis*, 28) *Litotes*
6. 'Figures based on Sound'	29) *Alliteration*, 30) *Onomatopoeia*, 31) *Pun*;
7. 'Figures based on Construction'	32) *Interrogation or Rhetorical Question*, 33) *Exclamation*, 34) *Hyperbaton or Anastrophe*, 35) *Prolepsis (Anticipation)*, 36) *Chiasmus or Inversion*, 37) *Hendiadys*, 38) *Tautology*, 39) *Pleonasm*, 40) *Ellipsis*, 41) *Asyndeton*, 42) *Polysyndeton*, 43) *Anaphora*, 44) *Epistrophe*, 45) *Anadiplosis*, 46) *Epanadiplosis*, 47) *Palilogy*, 48) *Catachresis*, 49) *Anacoluthon*, 50) *Aposiopesis*.

1. Figures based on Similarity

We have included five figures in the group of similarity, as written in the above chart, which again may be divided into two sub-groups on the basis of nature of similarity. While the first two, **simile** and **metaphor** are based on short comparisons, the remaining three figures 'allegory', 'parable' & 'fable' introduce long comparisons.

The division is as following:
Group I: (short comparison): (1) **Simile**, (2) **Metaphor**,
Group II: (long comparison): (3) **Allegory**, (4) **Parable**, (5) **Fable.**

Simile, Metaphor

(1) **Simile:** A figure of speech in which a likeness (similarity) between two things is stated in an explicit way; as,
"I wandered lonely as a cloud."
Here, we observe three things in the comparison made in the above sentence:

a. A comparison which is made between two different things (**'I'** & **'clouds'**; animate & inanimate.)

b. The comparison is made explicit with the help of the word, **'as'**, &
c. The <u>point of comparison</u> is *the state of loneliness* which is common in both to **'I'** (<u>the poet Wordsworth who is wandering 'alone'</u>) and the **cloud**, <u>floating in the sky alone.</u>

More examples:

1) 'The Assyrian came down like a wolf on the fold.' (Byron)
   - Here, a comparison is made between two different objects— **Assyrian** & **wolf**,
   - The comparison is made clear or explicit by the word, **'like'**, &
   - The <u>point of comparison</u> is the '*way' or 'manner of attack*'; the silent but steady attack on the enemy or target.

2) 'When the evening is spread out against the sky
   Like a patient etherized upon a table.' (T. S. Eliot)
   - A comparison is made between two different things (**'evening'** & **'patient'**)
   - The comparison is made explicit by the word, **'like'**, &
   - The <u>point of comparison</u> is their *'spreading darkness'*. As evening spreads darkness against the sky, so as 'a patient' is made insensible (read 'dark') on the table, applying ether, a chemical compound used as an early anesthetic. (a patient is being rendered insensible by means of ether, as by inhalation; the ***patient's becoming insensible*** is compared with <u>*darkness spread by the evening*</u>)

3) 'Her eyes as stars of twilight fair;
   Like twilight's too, her dusky hair.'
   - This is a simile too. In this figure a thing is likened to another in an explicit way. Here, we find two sets of comparison, *'eyes' and 'stars'* and another is *'hair' and 'twilight'*.
   - The comparison is made clear or explicit by the word, **'as'**,
   - Their points of comparison being *'fair of eyes like stars'* & *'dusky of the hair like twilight darkness'* —are stated respectively.

4) 'The soul was like a star, and dwelt apart.' —Wordsworth
   - This is a simile because an explicit comparison is made between two unlike objects 'soul' and 'star' in respect of brightness, and the comparison is made explicit by the word, *'like'*.

5) 'Like a child from the womb, like a ghost from the tomb,
   I arise and unbuild it again.' —Shelley

- o This is a simile too. In this figure a thing is likened to another in an explicit way. Here, we find two sets of comparison, *'I' (cloud) and 'child'* and *'I' (cloud) and 'ghost*.
- o In each case, the point of comparison which is 'suddenness' is clearly shown by the word, *'like'*.

6) 'For Natural Abilities, are like Natural Plants that need proyning by study'   —Bacon
   - o This is an example of simile. In this figure a thing is likened to another in an explicit way.
   - o Here, **'Natural Abilities'** and **'Natural Plants'** are compared. These are two unlike objects.
   - o The point of comparison is that both of them require 'proper nurture', and the similitude is, however, made explicit by the word, *'like'*.

More examples of 'Simile' (for your practice):

7) As dry as a bone; as proud as peacock; as light as a feather, etc. are examples of common similes we use in our everyday speech, and there are also others-
8) 'The champak odors fall,
               Like sweet thoughts in a dream' (Shelley)
9) 'Her locks were yellow a gold.' (Coleridge)
10) 'The holy time is as quiet as a Nun.'

Classification of Similes: Similes may, however, be long or short. On the basis, similes are classified as i) **Simple similes** (simple similes are shown above or so far) and **Epic similes** (which are again known as Homeric Similes, named after its introducer, Greek poet and philosopher, 'Homer'. However, in English there are lots of we find Homeric or so-called Epic similes in the writings of Milton (in his 'Paradise Lost' 'Paradise Regained'), Matthew Arnold (in his 'Shorab & Rustam'). Examples are withheld for the present.

(2) **Metaphor:** A figure of speech in which a likeness (or comparison) between two different things is stated which is implied, not clearly stated; as,

"He is the pillar of the state."

We observe three things:
a. A comparison is made between two different things (**'He'** & **'pillar'**)
b. The *comparison is implied, not clearly expressed* with such words; as, *'so'*, *'such'*, *'like'*, *'as'*, etc.

c.   However, *the point of comparison* which is distinct in the poet's thought only is about *the importance of the person in the state*, as a pillar for a construction or large building. He is such an important person of the state.

More examples:

1)   'He has a *stony heart*.'

o   Metaphor is used in the line. Here, a comparison is made between two different objects— **stone** & **heart**.

o   The comparison is implied, not explicit like a simile, &

o   The *point of comparison* is the 'hardness' of a stone and his heart, as the speaker thinks about him.

2)   'The *ship ploughs* the sea.'

o   A comparison is made between two different things ('the **ship**' & 'a **plough**')

o   The comparison is implied, not explicit like a simile, &

o   The point of comparison is 'the ability to force a way through'. As a farmer when ploughs, his plough makes a way through the land, so as a ship makes its way through the water when it sails on the sea.

3)   '*Life* is but an empty *dream*.'

o   This is a metaphor too. In this figure a thing is likened to another in an implied way.

o   Here, the comparison is made between **'life'** & **'dream'**.

o   The point of comparison is '*the vacuum in life*' what the poet thinks of himself or other as of 'our dream' contains nothing but vacuum of all thing.

4)   'The *camel* is the *ship* of the desert.'

o   This is a metaphor. In this figure a thing is likened to another in an implied way.

o   Here, the comparison is made between **'camel'** & **'ship'**, two unallied things.

o   The comparison is made which is implied, not explicit like in similes. However, the point of comparison (understood) is '*the only and main means of exporting things, as ship in the sea, so as a camel in the desert.*'

5)   '*Variety* is the *spice* of life.'

o   This is another example of metaphor. As food is tasteless without spices, so as 'varieties' in our life; without varieties in life, life becomes dull and fruitless (or at least, seems to be) boring to lead one. Excitement, adventure in doing new things, discovering new dimensions are the spices in our life.

- o Here, the comparison is made between **'variety *(in life)*'** & **'spice'**.
- o The point of comparison (which is '*seek for adventure, discovering new dimension*'), is, however, implied, not made clear as in similes.

6) 'The *ice mast* high came floating by.'   —Coleridge

- o This is a metaphor too. In this figure a thing is likened to another in an implied way.
- o Here, the comparison is made between **'ice'** & **'mast'**.
- o The point of comparison is '*coldness and stiff, lifeless*' what the poet thinks of the mast and ship without life in it. All are supposed to be dead in the ship that came floating by.

7) 'I will drink *life* to the *lees*.'   —Tennyson

- o Here is another metaphor. In this figure a thing is compared to another in an implied way.
- o Here, the comparison is made between **'life'** & **'lees'**.
- o The point of comparison is '*enjoying life in full fathom*' *like drink a bottle or cup to its less leaving no drops at the bottom'*. However, the point of comparison is implied, not clear, we made only an explanation.

8) '*She* seemed a splendid *angel,* newly drest.'

- o This is a metaphor too. In this figure a thing is likened to another in an implied way.
- o Here, the comparison is made between **'she'** & **'angel'**.
- o The point of comparison is '*looking very beautiful'*. *She looks like an angel in her new dress.* However, the point of comparison is implied.

More examples of 'Metaphor' (for your practice):

9) That reed was too frail to survive the storm of its sorrow.
10) The hockey–legged girls who laughed behind their hands.
11) *He* is the only *hope* of his family.
12) *Revenge* is a kind of wild *justice*.
13) He failed to *bridle* his *passion*.
14) I *drank delight* of battle with my peers.
15) A *dead silence* prevailed there.
16) He missed a *golden opportunity*.

Conversion of Simile & Metaphor

A simile and a metaphor differ only in form, but not in substance. Both are comparison between two unallied or two different things or objects. So, they can easily be transformed from one to other. Every simile can be compressed into a metaphor (as a metaphor is smaller in size than a simile), and every metaphor can be expanded into a simile (by using a marker of comparison; as— *like, as, so, such*, etc.), when the **point of comparison** will remain the same; as the followings:

1) The camel is the ship of the desert. (metaphor)
   - ✓ As the ship is used for crossing the sea, so is the camel used for crossing the desert. (simile)

2) Thy word is a lamp to my feet. (metaphor)
   - ✓ A lamp guides the feet of a traveler in darkness, so your words guide me action when I fall into a confused state. (simile)

3) The wish is father to the thought. (metaphor)
   - ✓ As a father begets children, so wish provides thoughts. (simile)

4) Variety is the spice of life. (metaphor)
   - ✓ As spice flavors food, so variety makes life enjoyable. (simile)

Allegory, Parable, Fable

(3) **Allegory:** A comparison between two unallied subjects is made through a narrative or story through numerous details, with a moral undertone (*so why it is also called a detailed comparison*).

So, allegory, like simile and the metaphor, is a comparison between two different objects. But with an allegory, the comparison is not short. It is made prolonged, through numerous details, as said in the definition.

Generally, *characters of an allegory portray human virtues or vices that play role like human beings and intended to give men a moral lesion.* However, the significance, instruction or lesion what it intends to provide, may have political, social or religious bearing. In simile, or metaphor, the comparison is made, is concise and short and have no such any color bearing.

Bunyan's "Pilgrimages' Progress" is a well-known allegory in English literature. It is apparently the story of a pilgrim, attempting to reach a distant place, through caves and pitfalls. But the moral it teaches is that a virtuous man or a pious Christian, in order to reach the place of God, or to be rewarded with the bliss of Heaven, must be ready to encounter various hardships, struggles in the journey of life. The perils of the road to Heaven are compared to the pitfalls of the road of a pilgrim along the way of his pilgrimage. Bunyan's 'The Pilgrim's Progress' is a religious or ethical allegory.

Langland's 'Piers Plowman', Spenser's 'Faerie Queene', Swift's 'The Tale of a Tub', 'Gulliver's Travels' are other best-known allegories in English literature.

(4) **Parable:** A parable is short allegorical story, with a moral. You can say a short version of an allegory. In a Parable, <u>animal characters are shown with human characters</u> to talk or converse with and the plot moves on. The moral of a parable lies side by side with the story, but sometimes it is given at the end.

'The Parable of the Sower', described in the New Testament may be referred to as a good example of parable, and the *Holy Bible* itself abounds in many parables in it.

(5) **Fable:** Like a Parable, a Fable is also a short story with a moral, but not often allegorical as the parable is. *The distinction of a fable is that in fables irrational animals are made to think, speak and act like men.* Animals, birds or other creatures are its characters to play all roles, not any intrusion of human beings in their world. **Aesop's "Fables"** are still known as one of the best Fables in the world. The Lion and the Mouse, The Hare and the Tortoise, and thus so many ones belong to Aesop's fables. George Orwell's 'Animal Farm' is a modern instance of the fictional fable to satirize the existing political and social state of our time

The above three are similar in their goal, to convey a moral lesion; but whereas in Parable and Fable the moral lesson is taught in a general way, in allegory, the lesion is more particular about the victory of certain virtue over certain vice.

2. Figures based on Difference or Contrast

Our idea about a thing becomes clearer if we see it against its contrast or difference; as, *'a bright object looks doubly bright when it is set against a black background'*, or *'a diamond appears to be highly glittering when placed against a black setting'*. So as, it happens to sentences like in the followings:

- ✷ 'Youth is full of pleasures; age is full of care.'
- ✷ 'She is carefully careless.'
- ✷ 'We fall to rise.', **etc.**

So, difference or contrast, like figures in similarity, helps us not only better understand of the thing but also make the sentence more effective, forceful or impressive than any other usual statement or question. Only we need to understand what figure suits to which kind of sentence.

However, the figures based on difference or contrast includes: -6) Antithesis, 7) Epigram, 8) Paradox, 9) Oxymoron, 10) Climax & 11) Anti-Climax.

Antithesis, Epigram, Paradox

(6) **Antithesis:** It is a figure of speech (the art of speaking or writing) in which contrasted words or ideas are placed against each other in the same sentence in the form of a balance for sake of emphasis on either of the ideas; as,

"United we stand, divided we fall."

Two contrasted ideas— 'United we stand' & 'divided we fall'—are set side by side, and they are contrasted to each other. And this combination of two contrasted ideas made the first part more forceful which the speaker or the messenger of the speech intends to convey or deliver, i.e. 'Unity is the strength'.

The characteristics, noted in an Antithesis:
a. Two contrasted ideas (by words) are set against each other,
b. The arrangement of words is made in a way to balance each other to produce two different ideas,
c. The inclusion of opposite is actually to make forceful the former idea (however, it may reverse, or intends to put emphasis on both parts of the sentence.').

More examples of 'Antithesis':

- 'Art is long, life is short.'
  - ➢ This is an Antithesis. Two contrasted ideas— **'Art is long' & 'life is short'**—are set side by side, intended to make the first part more forceful and clearer, i.e., 'the longevity of art', or to give emphasis on both 'the longevity of art' and 'the impermanence of life'. (*So, it is not bound always to give emphasis on former idea, but may also be on later part or on both parts.*)

- 'Better to reign in Hell than serve in Heaven.' (Milton)
  - ➢ This is an Antithesis too. Like the above, here too, two contrasted ideas— **'reigning in Hell' & 'serving in Heaven'**— are placed side by side, intended to give emphasis on 'the free will' or 'the love of freedom' of the speaker (here, 'Satan', the protagonist figure or character in Milton's "Paradise Lost".

- 'Give *every* man thine ear, but *few* thy voice.' (Shakespeare)
  - ➢ This is an Antithesis. Two contrasted ideas— *'lending of one's ear to every man'* is set against another *'speaking one's true thoughts only to a few'*. They are set in the form of balance and a term or word **'everyman'** of the first part is set against its opposite **'few'** in the last part of the sentence for sake of emphasis 'we should speak our true thoughts only to few'.

- 'To err is human, to forgive divine.' (Milton)
  - ➢ This is an Antithesis too. *'To err'* and *'to forgive'* — are placed side by side in the succeeding two parts of the sentence, intended to give emphasis on 'Forgiving is the divinity'.

- 'Made weak by time and fate, but strong in will.' (Tennyson)
  - ➢ This is an Antithesis too. Here two contrasted words or ideas are placed side by side in a balanced form for the sake of emphasis. In the above example, two contrasted words *'weak'* and *'strong'* — are placed side by side in the succeeding two parts of the sentence, intended to give emphasis on the entire proposition or idea that *the speaker's strength of will is not yet gone.*

- 'Man is a hater of truth, a lover of fiction.'
  - ➢ This is an Antithesis. Here, *'a hater of truth'* and *'a lover of fiction'* — are two contrasted ideas, placed side by side in the succeeding two parts of the sentence, intended to give emphasis 'the human nature that has fondness for fiction and dislike for facts'.

For your Exercise: **Find out 'Antithesis' from the followings:**
- Fool rush in where angels fear to tread.
- Marry in haste, repent in leisure.
- I never knew so young a body with so old a head. (Shakespeare)
- He was not the master but the slave of his speech.
- I must be cruel to be kind.
- To do a great right do a little wrong.
- God made the country; man made the town.
- A friend exaggerates a man's virtue, an enemy his crimes.
- It is a blessing and not a curse.

(7) **Epigram:** The epigram is an apparent contradiction in language which, by causing a temporary shock, rouses our attention to some important meaning underneath; as,

"Our antagonist is our helper."

Here, an apparent contradiction in language is produced by two words used in the sentence— **'antagonist'** and **'helper'** which are opposite in meaning. It rouses the thought *how an antagonist (an enemy) would be our helper (a friend)*, but after careful examination it strikes a deeper thought, 'when we face enemy or obstacles we come to know of our weakness and thereby we try to improve ourselves. Thus, an enemy also helps us, indirectly though. The deeper meaning, of course is the result of the processing of thoughts borne in the mind of the reader who reads the line and the writer intends that to produce by his arrangement of words in the line.

We observe three things in an epigram:
a. Two contrasted ideas (or words) are set against each other, like in an Antithesis;
b. The arrangement of words produces an apparent contradiction in language,
c. Close study rouses a striking thought or deeper meaning out of the line.

More examples of 'Epigram':

1) 'Our sweetest songs are those that tell of saddest thought.' (Shelley)
   ➤ This is an Epigram. There is a contradiction in language that said of *saddest thought' to be the sources of 'our sweetest songs'* and thus reveals a striking thought, though initially it seemed absurd. But the truth lies in it that *our saddest thought of bad experiences able to stir the deepest emotions in us* and which move the readers.

2) 'I am content, and I don't like my situation.' (Goethe)

> This is an Epigram too. Like the above, here too, a pointed expression to a significant level appears out through the apparent contradiction in the language—how even being content one cannot like his situation—strikes our thought. But after careful examination of the sentence, it makes clearer that _while contentment keeps one inactive, the sense of dissatisfaction can inspire hope and inflames one into activity._

3) 'Cowards die many times before their death.' (Shakespeare)

> This is an Epigram. There is a shocking contradiction—_how one can die many times_. But after careful examination of the sentence, it comes clearer _'cowards suffer continuously from the fear of death even before death comes to them.'_

4) 'The child is father of the man.'—Wordsworth

> This is an Epigram. _How a child to be the father of a man._ After careful study of the statement, it becomes evident, '_a present child is the father of a future man'_ and another '_a child character shows what the future man's father will be'._

5) "He makes no friend who never made a foe.'

> This is an Epigram. Behind the shocking contradiction at the initial stage the sentence makes clearer '_a man who does not mix with people neither makes a foe nor a friend.'_ And also '_through petty quarrels friendship is cemented.'_

6) 'The more a man loves, the more he suffers.'

> This is an Epigram. Loving is a beautiful feeling in men, but there lies also another truth, '_people suffer most from the cause of love.'_
>
> Thus, an epigram is always an example of brief and witty expressions that gives a shock at the initial stage but careful study reveals a deeper thought or truth, the writer or speaker intends to deliver.

7) "No man teaches well, who wants to teach."—Ruskin

> This is an Epigram.
>
> In an epigram, there is a contradiction in the apparent meaning of the language used, but there is an inner meaning.
>
> Behind the apparent contradiction there lies a deeper truth or meaning in the sentence 'that a man who wants to teach' cannot teach well'. This shocking expression, however, contains an underlying sense and aptly _suggests the failure of those who pride on their ability of teaching._

(Like Peter? However, how Peter dare!)

Find out the epigrams and give illustration against each:
8) In the midst of life, we are in death.
9) There is a pleasure in poetic pain.
10) Failure are the pillars of success.
11) The path of glory lead but to the grave. (Gray)
12) The blessedness of being little. (Shakespeare)
13) I can resist everything except temptation. (Wilde)
14) The busiest man has the amplest leisure. (Goldsmith)
15) Beware the fury of a patient man.
16) They always talk who never think.
17) More haste, less speed.
18) The king is dead, long live the king.
19) He is all fault who hath no fault at all.

<u>Distinction</u> between *Epigram* & *Antithesis*:

* The contradiction exists both in Antithesis & Epigram; but,
* The ***contradiction is real in Antithesis***. It is used in antithesis <u>for sake of emphasis on either of the ideas</u>; as,
  > ✓ Give me liberty or give me death.
* The speaker seeks for liberty through the line. It is emphasized by the contradiction produced by two opposite words— 'liberty' & 'death'.

* ***In epigram the contradiction is apparent***, there <u>lies a deeper or important meaning underneath the apparent contradiction</u>; as,
  > ✓ He who has never hoped can never despair. (Shaw)

* After close study, it comes evident it is hope, not fulfillment of something, that generates despair in the human mind.

(8) **Paradox:** In epigram, we find a contradiction in using the terms; in paradox, *the contradiction lies to our received thought, belief or opinion*; however, we finally meet or find out a novel truth, (i.e., a valid meaning) behind the apparent contradiction to our received thought. Let's read the definition of Paradox:

A statement or assertion which seems to be absurd at first reading or hearing for its use of terms contradictory to a received thought, but thereby we reach to a novel truth or a valid meaning, true to the practical sense; as,

"Nine soldiers out of ten are cowards."

Everybody believes a soldier to be brave one. Thus, the above line initially, gives us a shock at our first reading; for, **'how can soldiers be coward?** It conflicts with our received idea of soldiers whom we believe to be brave and fearless.

But soon, it reveals a truth, the soldiers are also human beings, made of flesh and blood, they also cherish love, hope, and they are also afraid of death. The line thus reveals a novel truth.

We observe these two things in a paradox:
a. It contains a contradiction which contradicts or conflicts to our received thought, belief or an idea; but,
b. It, finally, reveals a novel truth or a valid meaning to the real sense.

Note: to an extent, paradox and epigram are equivalent and same in use and application. In antithesis, we use opposite terms in two parts of the sentence. In paradox and epigram, the contradiction lies in using language or expression, while truth lies underneath or in our perception.

More examples of 'Paradox':
1) "There is no one so poor as a wealthy miser."
➤ This is a Paradox. The absurdity rouses when we read *'a wealthy miser to be very poor'*. Then our understanding reveals that there is *none so poor than a wealthy miser who bears suffering yet having huge wealth with him.*

2) 'The world will be saved by failure.'
➤ This is a Paradox too. *How does a failure take credit to save the world?* But after close analyses it reveals, *if the future world will really be imperiled by the inventions of successful scientists or by the whims of politicians, it (our earth) has no fear to be imperiled from the failures.*

3) 'Defend him from his friends.'
➤ This is another example of Paradox. Contradictory thought is there *'defend from friends.* But after analyses, it reveals a truth, *dangers mostly come from friends, known persons more than that of unknowns, for we hardly believe dangers to come from them, our friends or known ones.* A friend or near ones can harm you so easily than others, if he or they want.

Some more examples of 'Paradox'. Find out them and analyze:
4) "Sweet are the uses of adversity."

5) One of the greatest disadvantages of hurry is that it takes such a long time. **(Chesterton)**
6) The quarrels of lovers are the renewal of love.
7) The only way to get rid of a temptation is to yield to it. **(Wilde)**
8) Silence is sometimes more eloquent than words.

Oxymoron, Climax & Anti-Climax

(9) **Oxymoron:** It is a figure in which contradictory words are used side by side, (not in two parts, like in Antitheis) where the opposite word is used as an adjective or adverb to a noun or an adjective for striking effect to the meaning; as,

    1) "She was *regularly irregular* in her presence in the college."

➤ It is an example of Oxymoron. Two sharply contradictory words **'regularly'** and **'irregular'** are used side by side for the striking effect to the meaning of her *'irregularity of presence' which is so systematic that it will be no exaggeration to call it 'regular'*.

The two chief characteristics in an Oxymoron are:
a. Two sharply opposite terms or words are used side by side;
b. This arrangement of words is for a striking effect to the meaning that emphasizes a particular sense.

More examples of 'Oxymoron':

2) 'They have a *plentiful lack* of wit.' (Shakespeare)
➤ It is an example of Oxymoron. Two sharply contradictory words **'plentiful'** and **'lack'** are used side by side for the striking effect to the meaning of *'intensity of the lack of wit'*.

3) 'And all its *aching joys* are now no more.' (Wordsworth)
➤ In the above example two sharply contradictory words **'aching** and **'joys'** are juxtaposed. The expression seems absurd for we know joys to be pleasing, not aching. But here they are used to mean a particular sense i.e., *when joys are too intense, they cause sometimes aching, and often cause bring your tears.* However, this aching or tears is due to pleasures, extreme happiness, but not for sorrow.

4) 'Do that *good mischief* which may make this island (Thine) forever.'

> *'good'* and *'mischief'* are used side by side for the striking effect to the meaning of *'this mischief would be for a good cause'*. In the above line, the meaning is intended, *what is mischief to Miranda may be good to Caliban.*

5) 'Thus *idly busy* roll their world away.' (Goldsmith)
> This is an oxymoron.
> In the oxymoron, two contradictory words are juxtaposed to achieve impressiveness.
> Here *'idly'* and *'busy'*, two contradictory words are juxtaposed. An effect of impressiveness is thereby achieved to mean *there is no business at all, or the business is a fake one.*

6) 'Whose dread command is *lawless law.*' (Byron)
> This is an oxymoron.
> In the oxymoron, two contradictory words are juxtaposed to achieve impressiveness.
> Here *'lawless'* and *'law'*, two contradictory words are juxtaposed. An effect of impressiveness is thereby achieved *'there is no law at all in his command'.*

The distinction among *Antithesis*, *Epigram*, *Paradox* & *Oxymoron*

The contradiction exists in each of them; but

> **In Antithesis**, two contradictory ideas exist in two parts of the sentence for sake of emphasis on either of the ideas. Thus, the contradiction in Antithesis is real; as, "United we stand, divided we fall.".

> **In epigram** the contradictory lies in the used language or expression by using terms; however, there lies a deeper truth or important meaning underneath the apparent contradiction of expression; as, "Our antagonist is our helper."

> **In Paradox**, the sentence itself conflicts with a received thought, shocking at the first reading, however, finally that reveals a truth, a novel thought. *(To an extent, epigram and paradox are similar in use or application, and they can be used together)*, as, "The world will be saved by failure."

> **In Oxymoron**, <u>the contradictory words are used side by side</u>, neither they are used apart or in two different parts of the sentence nor the sentence itself conflicts, but <u>one opposite word is used against other</u> as an adjective or adverb to a Noun or an Adjective; as, *"Peter was carefully careless to each project."*

(10) **Climax:** It is a figure in which a series of words, phrases or ideas, is arranged in an ascending order of importance or emphasis. *Actually, the term, 'climax' has come from Greek word, 'Klimax' which mean 'ladder'. Just as a ladder is used to go up, so in climax we gradually rise from a less important idea to a more important one. (Or to say, ascending journey from 1ˢᵗ action through 2nd, 3ʳᵈ and thus to the last action in a series mentioned in a line. But the problem is they are not bound always to be actions.)*

In climax each succeeding idea is more striking and impressive than the previous one. As a result, the sense rises gradually, and gains impressiveness, importance, and force at every step, so why it is called 'climax'. For example,

"I came, I saw, I conquered."—at every step there is an increasing importance than the earlier one, or as 1ˢᵗ, 2ⁿᵈ, 3ʳᵈ action. (If I don't come, how can I see, and if I don't see or realize or understand the thing, how to conquer one?)

❑ **<u>Let's discuss its chief characteristics</u>**, though already mentioned through explanation:

a. It consists of a series of ideas, words, or phrases;
b. The least significant (which we consider the first action of a series) of them comes first and the most significant one comes last.
c. The purpose of Climax is to gain a succeeding impressiveness or effect to an expression.

More example of Climax:

1) 'A heart to resolve, a head to contrive, and a hand to execute.' (Gibbon)
   > This is a climax. In this figure the words or ideas — resolution, planning & execution— are arranged in ascending order *to emphasis 'the order of actions from resolution to execution'.* Thus, the sentence gets more impressiveness than merely mention one.

2) 'Vice is a monster whom we first endure, then pity, then embrace.'
   > This is a climax. In this figure the three ideas — enduring, pitying & embracing— are arranged in an ascending order *to*

*emphasis 'the order of ideas of **endurance, feel pity** and **embrace**' in which at every step the idea becomes more impressive & important than the earlier mentioned.*

3) The state of societies in large cities necessarily produces luxury; luxury gives birth to avarice; avarice begets boldness; and boldness is the parent of depravity and crime.'
   - ➢ This is a climax. In this figure the words or ideas — *luxury leading to avarice, to boldness, to depravity and crime—* are arranged in ascending order of importance or gradation to the final step of committing a crime.

4) To strive, to seek, to find, and not to yield. (Tennyson)
   - ➢ This is a climax. In this figure the words or ideas — *strive, seek, find and not to yield* — are arranged in ascending order of importance for impressiveness 'not to yield'.

5) 'Some books are to be tasted, others are to be swallowed, and some few to be chewed and digested.' (Bacon)
   - ➢ This is a climax. In this figure the words or ideas — some book to be *tasted, swallowed, chewed* and *digested'* — are arranged in ascending order of importance for impressiveness.

6) 'We'll hear him, we'll follow him, we'll die with him.'—Shakespear
   - ➢ This is a climax. In this figure the words or ideas arranged in an ascending order of importance.

     Here, *'to hear', 'to follow' and 'to die with him'—* are arranged in ascending order of importance or gradation *'**hear→follow→** and **die** with him.*

For your exercise: *Find out the climax and give illustration against each of them:*

7) Simple, erect, severe, austere, sublime.
8) [of Death] Black it stood as Night, fierce as ten Furies, terrible a Hell. (Milton)
9) What a piece of work is man! How noble in reason, how infinite in faculties! In action, how like an angel! In +apprehension, how like a god! (Shakespeare)
10) As Caesar loved me, I weep for him; as he was fortunate, I rejoice at it; a he was valiant, I honor him; but as he was ambitious, I slew him. (Shakespeare)
11) He was a thief, a plunderer, an assassin.

(11)　**Anti-Climax:** Anti-climax is a figure, opposite of climax, which consists in a sudden fall from lofty to mean; from high to low; from serious, elevated to the commonplace or trivial reference of subject matter, which produces a comic, ludicrous or satiric effect.

For example, in the following sentence-
"He lost his wife, his child, his goods, and his dog at one fell swoop"- we notice that there is *__a sudden descent__* from reference of subject matter *__regarding importance__*, from his *'lost his wife and son'* to *'goods and dog'*. It produces a comic effect.

Therefore, it can be said, anti-climax sometimes is purposely used, to produce the ludicrous effect, vastly in satiric, mock-heroic or epic poems or in drama, essays, etc.

❑ **The chief features of an anti-climax are—**
a.　Like climax, it is also, consists of a series of words, phrases or ideas;
b.　They are arranged in descending order of importance, i.e., the most impressive comes first and the least impressive come last;
c.　The purpose is to produce a ludicrous effect, to provoke laughter.

Study the examples of Anti-climax:

1)　If parts allure thee, think how Bacon shined
　　The wisest, brightest, meanest of mankind. (Pope)
➤　This is an anti-climax. You will notice *a sudden descent from the sublime to the ridiculous*. Here, the most impressive idea comes first and the least comes last. The final term 'meanest of mankind' weakens the sense of seriousness that was introduced at the beginning 'the wisest', and this change excites our laughter.

2)　True Jedwood justice was dealt out to him. First came the execution, then the investigation, and last of all the accusation. (Macaulay)
➤　This is an anti-climax. You will notice the reference of last action 'execution' at first, when it should be at last, and gradually we reach to the reference of thing that should come first in the series. *The purpose is to ridicule 'the justice'.* The lines raise a satiric tone.

3)　'Who in the course of one revolving moon / Was lawyer, statesman, fiddler, and buffoon.' (Dryden)
➤　This is an anti-climax.
　　An anti-climax consists in the sudden fall from the lofty to the man thought for a comical or contemptuous effect.
　　　　Here is the *fall from 'lawyer' and 'statesman' to 'buffoon'* is comical and for contemptuous effect.

4) 'She lost her husband, her children and her handkerchief.'
➢ This is an anti-climax.
In an anti-climax, there is a sudden fall from lofty to the mean thought with a view to exciting ridicule or laughter.
Here *from 'husband' and 'children', there is a sudden fall to 'handkerchief'*, and the purpose is to excite contempt for the woman concerned.

For your Exercise: *Point out the Anti-climax or Bathos in the following examples, and illustrate each one:*
5) 'Here thou great Anna! Whom three realms obey, / Dost sometimes counsel take—and sometimes tea.' (Pope)
6) 'What female heart can gold despise? / What cat's averse to fish?' (Gray)
7) 'Forgets her prayers or miss a masquerade.' (Pope)
8) 'Poets and pigs are not appreciated until they are dead.'
9) 'Ye Gods! Annihilate but Space and Time, / And make two lovers happy.' (Pope)

3. Figures based on Association

The term **'association'** means **'connection' or 'linked with'**—parts, organs with the whole. We often find two objects which are closely connected with each-other; as, 'a pen with a writer', 'a sword with a soldier', 'a stethoscope with a doctor', 'a scythe with a farmer', 'a needle with a tailor', 'a claw hammer with a carpenter', 'a treadle wheel with a potter', 'a beautiful woman or scholar with their pride', 'a wealthy man with his pride, 'a wise with his gentleness', 'a sail with the ship', etc.

As the above ones where two things are closely associated, as we think of, we may say anything while mean another. Study the examples:
a) 'Pen is mightier than the sword'—to mean 'writing is more influential than fighting';
b) 'I need ten hands', to mean 'I need ten men'.
c) 'The press enjoys a great power in the country.', to mean 'the power of media (or, newspaper).'

Sometimes, this link or association is strong as between *'hands and men'*, but sometimes they are loosely connected too, as *'press and newspaper'*. We have included the figures based on associations are—9)

Metonymy, **10)** *Synecdoche,* **11)** *Hypallage or Transferred Epithet, &* **12)** *Allusion.*

Metonymy, Synecdoche,

(12)   **Metonymy:** It is a figure in which the name of one thing is substituted for another with which it is loosely associated; as,

- "He is ruined by the bottle."
- ➢ In the above sentence, we get an example of Metonymy, for here the name of one thing ('bottle') is substituted for that of another (drink) associated with the former. The nature of the relation is loose one.

- "The crown passed a law."
- ➢ In the above example the word 'crown' is the accompaniment of the king, but by the word we generally mean the 'king' himself. Here too, the nature of the relation is loose one. They relation is external and the two things can be physically separated from each other without any harm.

The chief characteristics of a Metonymy: —
   a.   One object is named but another is meant;
   b.   The two things are loosely connected or related;
   c.   They can be separated physically without any harm.

Study the **Varieties of Metonymy:** The figure Metonymy has several varieties, each of which is determined by the particular type of substitution (of one thing for another) used in this figure. These varieties are discussed below-

A. The place for its production: (P):
   → 'All Arabia (i.e., the perfumes of Arabia) breathes from yonder box.' /
   → O for a beaker full of the warm South (i.e., wine made in the southern part of Europe)

B. The passion for the object inspiring it: (P):
   → 'He is the pride (i.e., object of pride) of his country.'
   → Shakespeare was England's glory (object of glory).

C. The author (or maker) for his work: (A):
   → 'He was reading Browning (i.e., his works or poetry)'.

→ He went down with a Davy (a safety lamp, invented by Humphrey Davy).

D. The act of the object inspiring it: (A):
→ 'The principles of liberty were the scoff (i.e., object of scoff) of every grinning courtier.'
→ 'People's prayer (the act of pray) saved him.'

E. The container for the thing contained: (C):
→ 'The cup (i.e., its tea) cheers them all.'
→ The bottle (drinks) ruined him to death.
→ The kettle (water) boils.

F. The cause for the effect: (Ck):
→ 'They are basking in the sun (to mean 'sun-shine', it is used 'sun', the cause of sun-shine.)'
→ He writes a good hand ('hand-writing' to mean).

G. The effect for the cause: (Egg):
→ 'The bright death (i.e., the sword, the cause of death) quivered at the victim's throat.'
→ 'Grey hairs (old age, their cause) should be respected.

H. The symbol for the thing symbolized: (Sandwich &):
→ 'From the cradle (i.e., infancy) to the grave (i.e., death).'
→ Scepter (Governors) and crown (kings) must tumble down.'

I. The instrument or organ for the agent (Ice-cream):
→ 'The pen (i.e., writer) is mightier than the sword (i.e., soldier.')
→ The press (newspapers, journalists) and the platform (orators) can greatly move the people.

❑ Remember the sentence "PACk Egg, Sandwich & Ice-cream" to remember the different varieties of Metonymy where the Capitals stand for names of varieties of Metonymy. 'PAC' will have to be counted twice.

(13)　**Synecdoche:** It is a figure in which a thing is substituted for another with which it is closely or intimately associated.
　　Varieties: Like Metonymy, a Synecdoche too has varieties. Study the followings:

A. **A part for the whole:** In this variety, we name a part of a thing but mean the entire or whole; as,

→ Give him a daily **bread** *(i.e., 'food')*, he will assist you in your works.

→ He engaged the best **brains** *(i.e., 'intelligent men')* to find out a solution.

→ A fleet of fifty **sail** *(i.e., 'ships')* went forward to meet the challenge.

→ Uneasy lies the **head** *(i.e., 'king')* that wears the crown.

→ **Silver and gold** *(i.e., 'riches')* I have none.

→ She is a woman of eighty **winters** *(i.e., 'years')*.

→ I have no **roof** *(i.e., 'houses')* to take shelter under.

B. **The whole for a part:** *In this figure an entire thing is mentioned to indicate only a part of it, e.g.,*

→ Wake the **purple years** *(i.e., 'spring')*. (Gray)

→ The lavish moisture of the **melting years** *(i.e., 'rainy season')*. (Thomson)

→ All rejoice at the coming of the **smiling year** *(i.e., 'spring')*.

→ Cold greets the **falling years** *(i.e., 'autumn')*.

C. **The abstract for the concrete:** *In this variety an abstract quality is mentioned which actually means for a concrete one, e.g.,*

→ I am out of **humanity's** *(man's)* reach. (Cowper)

→ Let not **ambition** *(ambitious men)* mock their useful toil. (Gray)

→ All the **rank and fashion** *(men of rank and fashion)* came out to see the sight.

→ He is no **authority** *(man having authority or power)* in this matter.

→ All the **beauty** *(beautiful women)* and the chivalry *(knights)* assembled there.

→ He is a walking **lie** *(liar)*.

→ All the **wit & learning** *(witty and learned)* were invited there.

D. **The concrete for the abstract:** *In this variety concrete object is mentioned to indicate or mean an abstract quality; e.g.,*

→ There is the mixture of the **tiger** *(cruelty)* and the **ape** *(sensuality)* in the character of a French man. (Voltaire)

→ He allowed the **father** *(fatherly feelings)* to be overruled by the **judge** *(the sense of justice)*.

→ Wisely kept the **fool** *(folly)*. (Dryden)

→ There is a good idea of **the fox** *(cunning)* in that old man.

→ None felt the **poet** *(poetic feelings)* in him.

E. A species for the genus: A species is mentioned to mean the genus (like an individual for the class or group; a part for the whole, etc.); as,

→ No, rather I abjure all **roofs** (*houses*) and choose to be a comrade with the **wolf and the owl** (*beasts and birds*). (Shakespeare)
→ **Princes and lords** (*aristocrats*) may flourish or fade, an art never.

F. The genus for a species: The large or extended is mentioned to mean a species or part. It is like the whole for the part; as,

→ Drink, pretty creature (lamb) drink. (Wordsworth)
→ He was killed in action (battle).
→ Vessels (ships) large may venture more, but little boats should be kept on shore. (Franklin)

G. An Individual for the class: This figure is like 'the part for the whole', or 'a species for the genera'. In this figure we name a person but mean for 'a class like that one'. In the words of Nesfield, 'a Proper Noun is used as a Common Noun'; as,

→ He was a Solomon of his age. (a wise king; one of the men noted for 'wisdom')
→ Let him be Caesar. (Caesar: noted for his heroic qualities)
→ A Daniel came to judgment! (a wise and impartial judge)
→ One mute inglorious Milton (a great poet) here may rest, / Some Cromwell (a great patriot) guiltless of his country's blood. (Gray)

H. The material for the thing made: In this variety the material with which something is made is mentioned for the thing itself, e.g.,

→ Glance on the stone (monument) where our cold relics lie. (Pope)
→ He was clad in steel ((armor)
→ The marble (statue) speaks.
→ His canvass (paintings) drew praise from all.

❑ **Memory-aid:** Remember the phrase, **"PASs IMpassable"** to remember the different varieties of Synecdoche where the Capitals stand for names of varieties of Synecdoche. Remember 'PAS' along with their reverse figures, like the followings:

- P= (i) Part for the whole, (ii) Whole for the part;
- A= (i) Abstract for the concrete, (ii) Concrete for the abstract;
- S= (i)Species for the genus, (ii) Genus for a species;
- I= Individual for the class,
- M= Material for the thing made.

Transferred Epithet (Hypallage) & Allusion

(14)   Hypallage or Transferred Epithet: It is a figure in which an epithet (i.e., *an adjective denoting a special quality*) is transferred from the object to which it properly belongs to another with which it is mentally associated.

In the words of Webster, "it is a figure in which there is a **transference of attributes** from the proper subject to others." Study the example:

1) "He is now counting his days of in the condemned cell."
We find an epithet **'condemned'.** It is used with **'cell'** to which it does not really actually belong to; it *properly belongs to the subject* **'He'** (He is condemned due to his spending days in the cell.)

Study the characteristics:
a. An epithet is transferred from its proper subject to another,
b. Such shifting takes place as they are closely associated,
c. The epithet in most cases is transferred from a person to a thing.

2) 'The ploughman homeward plods his weary way.' —Gray
This is a transferred epithet. Here, the epithet or the adjective **'weary'** is used with **'way'** when it actually belongs to the **'ploughman'** who is weary or tired.

3) 'The holy anger and pious grief.
He solemnly cursed that rascally thief.'   —Barham
This is a transferred epithet.
In a transferred epithet, an epithet is transferred from the word to which it belongs properly to another associated with it in the mind of the speaker or author.
Here, the epithets or adjectives **'holy'** & **'pious'** which properly belongs to the man, i.e., they actually should describe the man, are transferred to **'anger'** and **'grief'**, respectively which are other two states of the man which the man feels.

More examples of Transferred Epithet:
4) *He* lay all night on a *sleepless pillow.*
5) The *murmurous haunt* of *flies* on summer eves. (Keats)
6) Winter kept *us* warm, covering/ Earth is *forgetful snow.* (T.S. Eliot)

7) *We* passed a ***restless night***.
8) *He* spent a ***happy day***.
9) *He* spent a ***sleepless night***.
10) *I* spent an ***anxious morning***.
11) A ***sleepless pillow*** was pressed by both; an ***anxious morning***
    slowly dawned. (Reynolds) (which belong to 'He')
12) Where lay the ***mighty bones*** of ***ancient men***.

(15) **Allusion:** It is a figure in which an indirect reference of a significant event or well-known person, place (of history, legend or mythology) is made through the arrangement of words; as,

1) 'This is the same bog where armies whole have sunk.'—
    This is an Allusion.
    In an Allusion, a word or expression <u>refers to</u> a well-known incident of the past, some legend or the writing famous, or saying of some great man, or some great character.
    The above line *<u>refers to</u> **great Serbian bog*** mentioned in Milton's
    'Paradise Lost'.

2) 'This is the place where five brothers with their mother were tried to burn to death.'
    This is an Allusion.
    In an Allusion, a word or expression refers to a well-known incident of the past, some legend or the writing famous, or saying of some great man, or some great character.
    The above line *<u>refers to the great incident in</u> **'Mahabharata'*** where Five Pandavas with their mother were tried to burn to death.

3) 'It was the battlefield where hundred princes lost their all only to five under the blessing of Lord Krishna.'
    This is an Allusion.
    In an Allusion, a word or expression refers to a well-known incident of the past, some legend or the writing famous, or saying of some great man, or some great character.
    The above line *refers* <u>the war of 'Kurukshetra'</u> *From 'Mahabharata'* where hundred princes of Kourava lost their lives in the hands of five brothers of Pandavas.

4) 'It is the lake where God asked his son, 'What is Dharma?''
    This is an Allusion.
    In an Allusion, a word or expression refers to a well-known incident of the past, some legend or the writing famous, or saying of some great man, or some great character.

The above line *refers an incident of 'Mahabharata'.*

5) 'And that one talent which is death to hide.'   —Milton
   This is an Allusion.
   In an Allusion, a word or expression refers to a well-known incident
   of the past, some legend or the writing famous, or saying of some
   great man, or some great character.
   Here the term, 'one talent', refers to the '**Parable of Talents**',
   narrated by Jesus Christ to his disciples.

4. Figures based on Imagination

Oscar Wilde states *'a poor man is not he who has no money but he
who has no imagination.'*

Human imagination is one of those qualities that differ a man from any
other animal. The poets, writers as well as philosophers and artists from
different fields are those ones who have given their masterpieces being
enriched in imagination. Imagination is that instrument that makes a
sentence always beautiful; as,

'Misfortune has struck me hard.'
'Fortune smiles on me.'

Here, '**Misfortune**' & '**Fortune**' are regarded (imagined) to be acting
like a 'a human being' who has the ability to strike a man or to give a
smile. The figures that have been included in the class of Imagination
are as the following:
- Personification,
- Personal Metaphor,
- Pathetic Fallacy,
- Apostrophe,
- Vision,
- Hyperbole

Personification, Personal Metaphor

(16)   **Personification:** It is a figure in which inanimate object or
   abstract ideas—are endowed with the attributes of living beings.
1) "Fortune is merry."   --in the statement we get an example of
   personification. Being merry is an attribute of a living being, like a

person; but here that quality is invested upon an idea, 'fortune' as it has sensibility and it can think & feel happy or merry.

2) "Let the floods clap their hands." --It is a human being who can clap his or her hands. That quality has attributed to 'floods' which is an inanimate object. It is another example of Personification.

3) "Opportunity knocks at the door but once." --An abstract idea 'opportunity' has been attributed with the quality of having the ability to knock at the door, and thus it is another example of Personification.

Note: The personified idea or object is often written in a capital letter, when it is considered as a Proper Noun.

The chief characteristics of a personification:
a. Only inanimate objects (of Nature) or abstract ideas are taken into consideration,
b. These are endowed with the personality of a living beings and they are invested with the attribution of human feelings as they can think, feel or act etc.

More Examples of Personification:

4) "Fear at my heart, as at a cup, / My life-blood seemed to sip." (Coleridge)
➢ This is an example of personification. In this figure, an abstract idea 'fear' is endowed with the personality or attribute of a living being. Here, it is of a tiger (it is a tiger's ability to sip blood, not of a human being, of course.)

5) 'But Patience, to prevent that murmur, soon replies.'—(Milton)
This is an example of personification. In this figure, an abstract idea 'Patience' is endowed with the personality or attribute of a living being, that as it can reply.

6) 'Great pines groan aghast'—(Shelley)
This is an example of personification. In this figure, the tree (not a human being) **'pine'** [tree] is endowed with the human quality or attribute as that can **'groan'** like a human being.

7) 'The thirsty earth soaks up the rain.
And drinks and gapes for drink again.'—(Cowper)

This is an example of personification. In this figure, an inanimate object '**earth**' is endowed with the attribute of a living being to feel '**thirsty**' and a it can '**drink' like a human being.**

8) 'And melancholy marked him for her own.' (Gray)
9) Nature might stand up / And say to the world, "This was a man." (Shakespeare)
10) Death lays his icy hands-on kings.
11) Where Darkness spreads her jealous wings.
12) Athens was the eye of Greece.
13) Fair laughs the Morn. (Gray)
14) Venice the eldest child of liberty. (Wordsworth)

(17)   **Personal Metaphor:** In Personal Metaphor there is Personification plus a Metaphor. It is a kind of Personification, for here too an inanimate object is invested with the attributes of a living being. Thus, in the expression, "The thirsty earth soaks up the rain." there is a comparison of earth with a thirsty animal as well as Personification when the earth is taken with the ability which can drink like an animal.

Read more examples:

1) "The fearful roar of the angry sea." --Roaring is an activity of a tiger. So, it is a Personification, but here is also <u>a comparison between the sea and the tiger on the point of roaring, making sound in their way to express anger.</u> So, it is an example of Personal Metaphor too, where is both Personification plus Metaphor.

2) "And the weary day turned to his rest, / Lingering like an unloved guest." --*How can day go to rest and be tired like an animal?* Day as well as Time never stops for anyone. But here, Day is compared to an animal who gets tired and go to take rest in the evening. And at the same time, the human attribute or the attributes of an animal is invested upon 'Day' in the lines. So, it is another example of Personal Metaphor.

3) "I bring fresh shower for the thirty flowers." (Shelley from 'The Clouds') --It is another example of Personal Metaphor where flowers feel thirsty like an animal, though a plant also need water, but the feeling has been attributed on it representing it a living being like a man or animal.

Pathetic Fallacy, Apostrophe,

(18)   **Pathetic Fallacy:** Like Personal Metaphor, Pathetic Fallacy is actually another variation of Personification.
Here too <u>a personal tribute is invested upon an inanimate object, though not on abstract idea.</u> Here, the *inanimate objects (of Nature) participate in some human concern by showing sympathy or antipathy to man* as in the following example:

1)   "Through torrid tracts with fainting steps they go / Where wild Altama murmurs to their woe." (Goldsmith)

➢   Here we get an instance of Pathetic Fallacy, for the poet represents the *river 'Altama' murmuring as out of sympathy for the woe of the emigrants* walking weakly along the torrid regions.

The chief characteristics of a Pathetic Fallacy are:
a.   It is concerned with Nature or inanimate objects, (not with abstract ideas, however);
b.   They are invested with human feelings of sympathy or antipathy;
c.   Nature or inanimate objects are shown to participate in some human concern either by showing sympathy or antipathy to man.

More Examples of Pathetic Fallacy:
2) "The river wept for the sorrow of the lady."
—This is a Pathetic Fallacy. Here, the nature in the form of *river feels sorrow for the distress of the lady*. An inanimate object 'river' is invested with human feeling of 'to feel sorrow' for other.

3) 'Armour rustling in the halls, /On the blood of Clifford calls.' *(Wordsworth)* — This is another example of Pathetic Fallacy in which an object *'armour' rustles showing antipathy, i.e., calling for Clifford's blood.*

4) 'Nature sighed for the woes of earth.'—Nature feels sorry for the distress of the earth.

5) 'The broad sun above laughed a pitiless laugh / When the Arab traders tried to cross the desert.'—The sun shows antipathy to the Arab traders.

(19)   **Apostrophe:** It is a figure in which <u>a short-impassioned address is made to a person, dead or absent, or to an inanimate</u>

<u>object, or to an abstract idea thinking as if, it is present and capable of understanding</u>.

Note: An Apostrophe needs not only strong emotion to be stirred up to imagine a non-living as living being and to address him as alive and present but also an elevated thought and language (diction) for composition & presentation.

Study the example:

1) "O Liberty! What crimes have been committed in thy name." — In the example, we notice <u>the speaker make an impassioned address to an abstract idea</u> (i.e., Liberty) and is imagined as if, it is present there to listen to him and understand. Intense emotion is coupled here with elevated thought and diction. Hence, it is a perfect example of an Apostrophe.

The chief characteristics of an apostrophe:
a. It involves a person, dead or absent, an inanimate object, or an abstract idea;
b. An address is made to any one of them, taking it live and present, and the address is short and impassioned;
c. The address reveals not only strong emotion but also elevated thought and diction.

<u>**More Examples of Apostrophe:**</u>

2) *"Frailty, thy name is woman!"* *(Shakespeare)*
—This is an example of Apostrophe. 'Frailty', <u>*a quality of woman, is addressed as a living being*</u> as if, it is present and listening to the speaker.

3) 'Milton! Thou shouldst be living at this hour.' (Wordsworth) — This is an apostrophe too. Here, the <u>*poet Wordsworth address another*</u>, Milton, a great poet, as he (Milton) is present and asking him impassionedly to live at that hour.

4) 'O cuckoo! Shall I call thee bird, / Or but a wandering voice?' *(Wordsworth)* —Another instance of apostrophe, where <u>*a non-human object (cuckoo) is impassionedly addressed*</u> as if, it is present there and the poet expresses his wonder on the bird's cry <u>*calling it 'a wandering voice.'*</u>

5) 'England! With thy faults, I love thee still.' (Byron) —addressing England as a lover.

6) 'O Wind, /If Winter comes, can Spring be far behind?' (Shelley)— asking a question to the 'Wind'.

7) 'O Death, where is thy sting? /O grave, where is thy victory?' — an eternal question, asked to Death & Grave as they are present and listening to the speaker.

Vision & Hyperbole

(20)   **Vision:** It is a figure which consists in **'*seeing*'** what is not actually seen. In the words of **Prof. Bain,** "It consists in the vivid representation of the absent as if present to the senses."

Note: Vision is different from Apostrophe in the sense that it does not consist in any address.

Nesfield identifies it with Prosopopoeia which he defines thus, "By this figure the speaker or writer *relates something in past* **or** describes some *anticipated future, but employs present tense instead of past or future,* in the attempt to make the event appear lifelike and present *occurring, passing or happening before our eye.*"

Notice the following example from Longfellow:

1) "But lo! In that house of misery / A lady with a lamp I see."
— In the above lines we have an example of vision. Because the poet sees before his very sight the presence of **'*the lady with a lamp in her hand*'** who is actually not present at least for the time, but the poet remembers her with the lamp life like, the past event is visualized as live by his imaginary sight with the choose of suitable diction and arrangement of words. (The vision of Florence Nightingale going from room to room with her message of hope and service to the wounded soldiers selflessly, out of love and care of a mother or sister to her ailing son or brother.)

More Examples of Vision:

2) "Pride in their port, defiance in their eye. / I see the lords of human kind pass by." *(Goldsmith)*

—It is another example of Vision. A vivid picture is raised so that one sees what is not actually seen.

3) 'And he plucked his cursed steel away, / Mark how the blood of Caesar followed it.' *(Shakespeare)*
— A vivid picture is drawn with the help of words, beautifully arranged in the manner the reader can see before him the sight, life-like and present, 'Julius Caesar in blood'.

4) 'Is this a dagger which I see before me, the handle towards my hand?' *(Shakespeare)* —The readers can visualize the sight before them and can realize the suffering, the repentance burning in the heart of Macbeth.

5) 'Me think I see in my mind a noble & puissant nation rousing herself like a strong man after sleep, and shaking her invincible lock.' *(Milton)* —We can perfectly see the sight in our vision or imagination, the vision of a rising nation. It is another perfect example of a vision.

(21) **Hyperbole:** It is a figure in which a deliberate overstatement is made for emphasis in favor of or against a person or thing. This figure is also known as **Exaggeration**. It may produce either seriousness or comic effect.

Exaggeration is a common habit of man. When we like a thing, we praise it too high; and if we dislike, we usually paint it most unfavorably. Hyperbole is the outcome of that tendency of man.

1) "Wish you millions of Happy Diwali."
2) "He offers you a thousand regrets." —
3) "I can bring Moon for you."
4) "If you say, I can jump to death for your love." – These are nothing but exaggerated statements. We wish one, mean one but tell of thousands, millions and of something that we can't do or follow any further than the statement.

The chief characteristics of a hyperbole:

a. A thing or a person is not presented in the normal state but in exaggeration;
b. The exaggeration occurs under the pressure of overpowering feeling;
c. Despite overstatement of expression, it is not to be taken too literally.

More Examples of Hyperbole:

5) 'Ten thousand saw I at a glance.'

This is a Hyperbole. Hardly ten thousand can be seen at a glance, or at least, who has counted the number. Simply, it is to express the ecstasy of the feeling, instigated by the sight or view.

6) 'This my hand will rather /The multitudinous seas incarnadine /Making the green one red.' *(Shakespeare)* — This is a Hyperbole. In this figure a deliberate overstatement is made for sake of emphasis. Here the exaggeration occurs when an assertion is made that a single hand can turn a green sea red.

7) 'Here is the smell of blood still; all the perfumes of Arabia will not sweeten this little hand.' *(Shakespeare)* —The infliction of heart out of the conscience, the repentance began to show its color through the speech of the speaker, Macbeth that not even all the perfumes of Arabia possess the capacity of sweetening one single hand stained by the blood of king Duncan.

8) 'My vegetable love should grow / Vaster than empires, and more slow.' (Marvell).'—The hyperbole is created or made when it is said or compared love with an empire.

9) 'Drink to me only with thine eyes.'

The ecstasy in love makes the statement a hyperbole when it is meant 'to drink love, i.e., to love the beloved through eyes.

10) 'In mathematics he was greater / Than Tycho Brache or Erra Pater.' *(Butler)* — When someone is compared and made greater than all great mathematicians in seconds, it is nothing but a case of Hyperbole.

11) 'Was this the face that launched a thousand ships / And burnt the topless towers of Ilium?' *(Marlowe)* —It is not the beauty of Helen but the war that was thrown between Troy & Sparta caused the thousand ships drawn or burn the towers of Ilium. This exaggeration of beauty of Helen is an example of Hyperbole.

12) 'I loved Ophelia: forty thousand brothers / Could not with all their quantity of love / Make up the sum.' (Shakespeare).'—Forty thousand brothers' love can't make up the sum of the speaker's love for Olivia—is nothing but another example of Hyperbole.

5. Figures based on Indirectness

We often express an idea directly. But sometimes we also want to express an idea or a thing in an indirect way to avoid harshness (of the speech) and to serve our purpose (to deliver message agreeably). It also achieves a poetic effect. Read the following example:

'He breathed his last the other day.'

The speaker means to say, 'He **died** the other day'. It is said somewhat agreeably, in order to avoid the harshness of the message of someone' death, when it is said 'he breathed his last'.

An affirmative idea can also be expressed indirectly with the help of Negative of its contrary; as, to mean *'many'*, we may use, *'not a few* (in place of 'many) *came to enjoy the show.*

The figures included in this class are:
1) Innuendo, 2) Irony, 3) Sarcasm, 4) Periphrasis, 5) Euphemism, 6) Meiosis, & 7) Litotes.

Innuendo, Irony, Sarcasm

(22) **Innuendo:** It is a figure in which something unpleasant or damaging is artfully hinted instead of being plainly stated. It is also known as Insinuation.

Study the example:
1) I do not consult a physician, for I hope to die without them. (Sir William Temple)

- Here the insinuation is that physicians more frequently send patients to death (if not by medicine, through prolonged tests and diagnostic process that left people for none [make them without wealth), when they should save their lives and also wealth from unnecessary waste.])

- The damaging remark for the reputation of doctors is made or hint indirectly than plainly stated. This indirect statement is called an Innuendo.

Note the characteristics:
a. A damaging remark is intended against a person or institution,
b. It is not plainly stated but only suggested in an oblique way.
c. The suggestion may be real or unreal. Often a hostile feeling for the men or against institution, is the cause behind an Insinuation.

<u>More examples of Innuendo</u>:

2) The picture is splendid as the artist is an octogenarian.
   > *This is an Innuendo. In this figure something damaging is suggested instead of being plainly stated.*
   Here the insinuation is that the picture deserves no praise or attention since an artist loses all his creative power in his eighty.

3) If he knew a little law, he would know somewhat of everything.
   > *The implication is that since he has not mastered his own subject, he can know only a little of other subjects.*

4) The frame of the picture is excellent indeed.
   > *The implication is that only the frame, not the picture, is excellent.*

5) A word to the wise is sufficient.
   > *The implication is that only the ignorant who requires words to be repeated.*

6) The hungry judges soon the sentence sign, / And wretches hang that juryman may dine.
   > *The implication is that dining is more important to judges than the fate of the accused.*

7) He quarrels with everybody but he is a sportsman.
   > *The implication is that though a sportsman is expected to be fair and forgiving, he quarrels frequently with everyone.*

8) The author's book will live at least a year.
   > *The implication is that the book is worthless and it can live for a year at the maximum.*

9) I shall lose no time in reading your book.
   > *The implication is that the book is worthless and it does not deserve time to be spent on.*

10) My friends were poor but honest.
   > *The implication is that poor people are generally dishonest.*

11) Such treatment I did not expect, for I never had a patron before. (Dr. Johnson)
   > *The implication is that a patron, far from assisting an author, treats him coldly and with indifference.*

(23)   **Irony:** It is a figure in which the very opposite of what is stated is meant or intended. In Irony we state the contrary of what we mean; as,

1)   'And Brutus is an ***honourable*** man.' (Shakespeare)
➢   Here Antony utters the word 'honourable' but the very taunting tone of his utterance indicates that it means just its contrary, i.e., ***dishonourable***.

2)   'No doubt ye are the people, and ***wisdom will die*** with you.'
➢   This is too an Irony. Here the word 'die' signifies its opposite—'not die', for the speaker emphasizes that wisdom will not die with them, as they are actually ***fools***.

Note the chief characteristics:
a.   Something is said but its contrary is meant.
b.   Apparently, it says of commendation but really it wants to hurt (hurting the target person or thing in an indirect way).

More examples of Irony:
3)   The brotherly love *(i.e., hatred)* of our enlarging Christianity is proved by the multiplication of murder. (Ruskin).
➢   *It is hatred not brotherly love of Christianity that multiplies murder.*

4)   I thank *(i.e., blame)* thee, Jew, for teaching me that word. (Shakespeare) (*'I like to blame you for teaching me that word'.)*

5)   With his usual punctuality *(i.e., lateness)* the boy entered into the class after the roll-call. (*The boy was late in the class, so...*)

6)   A very fine friend *(i.e., not a friend like)* you were to forsake me in my trouble. (*A true friend does not forsake one in trouble or danger.*)

7)   The reporter overwhelmed me by his beautiful *(i.e., detesting or irritating)* ignorance. (Kipling)

8)   The operation was successful though *(i.e., unsuccessful that)* the patient died. (*If the operation was successful the patent would not die.*)

(24)   **Sarcasm:** It is a figure in which a statement is made in such a way as to excite contempt, ridicule or scorn.

In sarcasm a man does not intend to mean the contrary what he says. He says what he means (a direct attack), but in a way to excite contempt or ridicule. Sarcasm exposes follies or weaknesses of a character in a bitter tone and ill-mannered. Its motive is to inflict pain.

Sarcasm is _neither Innuendo, nor Irony, but the between two_; as,

1) The Jews said of Christ that He saved others, but could not save Himself.

➤ This is an example of Sarcasm. The attack is direct on Christ; the indirect indication is, the speaker does not believe in His Godliness. The comment inflicts pain not only Jesus Christ (though hardly possible Who is above all these) but also all Christians who, like the writer himself, believe in His great cause.

Note: Sarcasm along with Innuendo, Irony, Wit—is vastly used in Satire, a generic name for a type of writing, as Hyperbole is seen in dramas & romantic poems enormous.

The chief characteristics:

a. In sarcasm, a direct attack is made against a person or thought, its purpose is to inflict pain.
b. It is always bitter and ill-mannered language used by different characters in dramas or novels, to excite contempt, ridicule or scorn for others.
c. There is no cleavage between what is stated and what is meant or intended, and thus it is different from irony.

More examples of Sarcasm:

2) His bark is worse than his bite.
➤ _The derision excites contempt for the man because of his habit of using harsh words._

3) Is not a patron, my lord, one who looks with unconcern on a man struggling for life in the water, and when he has reached the ground, encumbers him with help? (Dr. Johnson)
➤ Dr. Johnson's contempt has been directed toward the patron who show indifference to the writers at the initial stage, but when he has got success, they come forward for their help. The statement excites contempt for them and the purpose is to inflict pain.

4) Certainly, God did not make man and leave it to Aristotle to make him rational. (Locke)

➢ The derision is made to attack on Aristotle and its purpose is to excite contempt for him.

5) Christianity does not mean carrying the cross on the bosom and crucifying Christ at every step.
➢ The direct attack is made on those Christians who demand themselves to be Christians by customs and carrying cross mark on their bosom when they hardly follow Jesus' principles.

6) As for modern journalism, it is not my business to defend it. It justifies its own existence by the great Darwinism principle of the survival of the vulgarest. (Wilde.)
➢ —it is an attack on all those people who are indifferent to injustice occur before them, and it is clear when the writer used the phrase, *'the survival of the vulgarest.'*

Periphrasis, Euphemism,

(25) **Periphrasis:** It is a figure in which something is stated in a roundabout way instead of being expressed in a direct and brief manner. It is also known as **Circumlocution.**

In this figure many or very long words are used where that could be expressed with a few or simple words; as,
1) Her olfactory system was suffering from a temporary inconvenience' (simply it means, 'her nose was blocked').
➢ And thus, long words or certain phrase are used in place of some common terms; as read some in the table:

Periphrasis	Common Terms	Periphrasis	Common Terms
The finny tribe	Fish	The bleating kind	Sheep
The penultimate month	November	The month of Christmas	December
The moving island of winter	Ice—bergs	The jewel of the head	eye

The chief characteristics:
a. Some fact or idea is expressed in a roundabout way.
b. This is frequently done to avoid common place terms and for achieving poetic effect.

More examples of Periphrasis with their meanings in bracket:

2) The cup that cheers but not inebriates. (Cowper)
   → *[The above statement is used simply to refer* 'a cup of tea.'*]*
3) He resembled the animal that browses on thistles.
   → [The above long expression is used only to mean 'he resembled an ass.']
4) The viewless couriers of the air. (Shakespeare)
   → [The above long expression is used only to mean 'winds.']
5) Those green-robed senators of mighty woods. (Keats) [i.e., 'oak trees']
6) Sleep the sleep that knows no breaking. (Scott) [i.e., 'death']
7) The shining leather that encased the limb. [i.e., 'boot']
8) His statement was purely an effort of imagination. [i.e., 'a fiction or falsehood']
9) The shining orbs [i.e., 'stars'] that decks the sky.
10) And mine eternal jewel. [i.e., 'soul'] / Given to the common enemy of man. [i.e., 'Satan']
11) The knightly growth that fringed his lips. [i.e., 'moustache']
12) The orbed maiden with white fire laden. (Shelley) [i.e., 'moon']
13) The million-coloured bow. (Shelley) [i.e., 'rainbow']
14) Then felt I like some watcher of the skies. (Keats) [i.e., 'astronomer']
15) Wandering near her secret bower. (Gray) [i.e., 'nest']
16) The great fierce fish that thirsts for blood. (Doyle) [i.e., 'shark']
17) The star that guides the mariner. [i.e., 'Pole-star']
18) Three core year and ten. [i.e., 'seventy']
19) To answer in the positive or negative. [i.e., 'to say yes or no']
20) When the ivy-top is heavy with snow, /And the owlet whoops to the wolf below, / That eats the she-wolf's young. [i.e., 'winter'] (Coleridge)

(26) **Euphemism:** It is a figure in which something offensive or harsh is stated in an agreeable or pleasant way. It is to *'say softly an unpleasant truth.'*

For example:

1) 'He perished on the scaffold.'
➢ This is an example of Euphemism. The unpleasant truth that *'he was hanged'* is said indirectly to soften the harshness to the listeners.

The chief characteristics:

a. A harsh or blunt thing is expressed in a pleasant or wild manner.
b. It is done in an indirect or roundabout way.

c. Its purpose is <u>*to share one's feelings*</u>, thus it is opposite of Sarcasm & Irony where the purpose is to inflict pain & damaging the opponent or target one's reputation.

Note: As *Euphemism* is directly opposite *of Sarcasm* in its purpose, *Meiosis* is the opposite of *Hyperbole* relating exaggeration.

More examples of Euphemism:

2) He is short in his accounts.
> *This is a Euphemism. A mild and pleasant expression is used for a harsh or blunt one that is* 'He is poor', *is softened by the use of an agreeable turn of phrase.*

3) The bank has stopped payment.
> *Here too a mild expression is used to soften down the harshness i.e.,* 'The bank has become insolvent'.

4) The light-fingered gentry (*i.e., pick-pockets*) relieved him of his purse.

5) You said what is not. (*i.e., you told a lie.*)

6) The gang relieved the house-holders of their ornaments and cash. (*i.e., robbed*)

7) 'Henry VIII was singularly unfortunate in all his relationships with women.' (*i.e., 'He divorced two and beheaded two more of his six wives.*)

8) The army made a strategic retirement. (*i.e., retreated*)

9) He has fallen asleep never to wake up again. (*i.e., died*)

10) They dropped down one by one. (*i.e., died*)

11) Goldsmith was little, pitted with small pox and awkward; and schoolboys are amazingly frank. (*i.e., they told it to his face without caring for his feelings.*)

12) He is not as truthful as one might wish him to be. (*i.e., liar*)

13) You are telling me fairy tale. (*i.e., lie*)

Distinction among— Sarcasm, Irony, Innuendo, Periphrasis & Euphemism

All the above figures are based on Indirectness. But they have differences, too. While ***Innuendo, Irony, Sarcasm,*** —the three figures are prompted by hostility, they are used for hurting one's feelings,
***Euphemism** is prompted by kindness, it wants to spare the harshness and indulge in share one's feelings of sadness, evident in its expression.*

There is also **Periphrasis** among these five, which is prompted neither by kind nor by hostile feelings, mainly it is used for literary effect.

❏ Sarcasm, Irony, Innuendo—are almost same, yet they have difference too.

➤ **In Sarcasm** the attack is direct, bitter, and personal. In it the speaker says what he intends.

➤ **In Irony** the attack is indirect and disguised; there is condemnation through apparent praise. In it the speaker intends exactly the opposite of what he says.

➤ **In Innuendo** too, the attack is indirect, for no direct charge is made; in its insinuation of an injurious nature is made artfully and not plainly.

Meiosis & Litotes

(27) **Meiosis:** In Hyperbole, an overstatement is deliberately made. Meiosis is just it's opposite term. Here we find an *understatement*.
<u>In Mciosis, an understatement is deliberately made to heighten the effect of something.</u>

1) I have a little bad news to give, 'The company has decided to suck off 30% of its employees soon.
   ➤ This is an example of Meiosis. A very bad news for the employees is said to be *'a little bad news'; for* 'What is little may be for the company, is very bad news for its employees.'
   The statement, even as an understatement of it, it does not decrease, rather enhances its (poetic) effect.

➤ **<u>The chief characteristics:</u>**
a. A deliberate understatement is made.
b. This understatement enhances the impression rather than decrease its importance to the hearer.

2) She was ***rather beautiful.***
   - ➤ *This is Meiosis. The statement deliberately represents her beauty as much less in magnitude or importance (by using the term 'rather' with the word 'beautiful) than she really is. However, we get the impression of the speaker what does he mean, 'She is really **very beautiful.'***
   - ➤

3) That was ***some opera***, thousands of audiences drew it every time.
   - ➤ *Actually, to mean **'great opera'.***

4) The royal procession was **rather** good. *(i.e., 'much good')*

5) It needs ***some (i.e., great)*** faith to believe in the transmigration of souls.

6) I will teach ***somewhat (i.e., much)*** that you will not behave such again with any other.

7) I cannot move now, for I am ***a little (i.e., very much)*** tired.

(28) **Litotes:** It is a figure in which <u>a strong affirmation is meant or intended by negation of its contrary</u>; as,

1) The show is ***not bad.*** (i.e., it means 'The show is ***quite good*** or i.e., 'very good.')
   The meaning ***'very good'***, a strong affirmation is expressed <u>by negation 'not' of its contrary 'bad'</u>. This is an example of Litotes.

   Note: Like Meiosis, Litotes is also a kind of understatement, <u>only difference is that, this do so by recourse to negation of strong affirmation</u>. Litotes is a variation of Meiosis.

The chief characteristics:
a. An affirmative idea (often a strong affirmation) is expressed.
b. This is done by the negation of the affirmative word's contrary.
c. The deliberate understatement enhances its importance rather than lessen down.

More examples of Litotes:
2) He is no fool.
   - ➤ *This is a Litotes. Here an affirmative idea **'he is wise'** is expressed or indicated by the negation 'no' of its contrary 'fool'.*

3) <u>No maiden's hand </u>is around thee thrown. (Scott)

➢ In this sentence too, a strong affirmative idea '**a strong male's**' (No maiden's hand means 'a strong male's) is expressed by negation of its contrary.

4) I _praise you not_. *(i.e., blame)*
5) He is _not the brightest_ man in the world. *(i.e., most stupid)*
6) He is a citizen of _no mean city_. *(i.e., great city)*
7) Myself not least, but honored of them all.
8) This is _no common_ speech. *(i.e., uncommon)*
9) I was _not altogether displeased_ at the discomfiture of a bad man. *(i.e., pleased)*
10) It amused the king _not a little_. *(i.e., great or much)*

Distinction among—Hyperbole, Euphemism, Meiosis, & Litotes

✓ **Hyperbole**—is based on _deliberate over statement_ for emphasis.

✓ **Meiosis & Litotes**—both rest upon _deliberate understatement_ to heighten the effect of something.

✓ **Meiosis** stays _affirmative_; **Litotes** _express strong affirmation by help of negative of its contrary_.

✓ **Euphemism** is used to _soften down the effect_, but

   ✓ **Hyperbole, Meiosis & Litotes** are _employed to emphasize the effect of the statement._

6. Figures based on Sound

• Sound, as we all know, has great value in our life. When properly worded the sound of a sentence can soothe our heart and fill our mind with inexpressible joy. In the same way when harshly worded the sound of a sentence can create a jarring effect on our mind.

• In rhetoric, rhetorician use this sound effect to meet their different purposes, to raise musical effect as well as to make their expression effective & impressive; as,

'**M**ost **m**usical **m**ost **m**elancholy'

— **is not there, same letter at the beginning of succeeding words?** And this raises a musical effect.

Note: The rhetoricians, orators or writers often play on the sound of words in their sentence, speech or line for the effective expressions.

The figures included in the class of Sound are as the followings:

a. Alliteration,

b. Onomatopoeia,

c. Pun or Paronomasia.

Alliteration, Onomatopoeia

(29)   **Alliteration:** It is a figure in which the *same sound, letter or syllable is repeated in a sequence of nearby words* (at the beginning of two or more words) for the purpose to bring a sensuous pleasure to the ear (as already said, sounds create musical effect); as,

1) "With **bl**ade, with **bl**oody **bl**ameful **bl**ade." —the sound of the letters 'bl' is repeated in the succeeding words of the line.
2) 'A*f*ter li*fe*'s *fit*ful *f*ever' —the letter 'f' is repeated and sounds the line musical.
3) '*Un*wept, **un**honoured, **un**sung' (Scott) —the syllable 'un' has been repeated in the succeeding words of the line.

The chief characteristics of Alliteration:

a.   There is repetition, either of sound, letter or syllable in nearby or in the succeeding words of a line.
b.   That create a musical effect, give sensuous pleasure to the ear and make the sentence impressive than normal sentence.

Variation of Alliteration

Alliteration has two main variations. They are a) ***Consonance*** & b) ***Assonance***

(A) **Consonance:** As we already said, Alliteration is the repetition of same sound, letter or syllable in nearby or succeeding words, Consonance is one where we find *repetition of 'a sequence of consonants'* but with a change in the intervening stressed vowel; as,
'**li**ve-**lo**ve, **lea**n-a**lo**ne, **pi**tter-**pa**tter', etc.

(B) **Assonance:** Assonance consists in the *repetition of identical or similar vowel sounds*, especially in stressed syllable, in a sequence of nearby words', e.g.,
"Thou foster ch*i*ld of **s**ilence & **s**low-t*i*me." (Keats)

The above two are variations of Alliteration. You may identify them as Alliteration only will be enough for high school students.

<u>**More examples of Alliteration:**</u>

4) *A*n *A*ustrian *A*rmy *a*wfully *a*rrayed.
5) *Ru*in seizes thee, *ruth*less king. (Gray)
6) A *f*air *f*ield *f*ull of *f*olk. (Langland)
7) In a *s*ummer *s*eason when *s*oft was the *s*un
              It *sh*aped me in *sh*rouds as I, a *sh*eep were. (Langland)

8) *A*pt *A*lliteration's *a*rtful *a*id.
9) *Gl*ittering through *gl*oomy *gl*ades.
10) The *f*air *b*reeze *b*lew, the white *f*oam *f*lew,
                          The *f*urrow *f*ollowed *f*ree.

11) *Al*one, *al*one, *al*l, *al*l *al*one,
                          *Al*one on a *wi*de, *wi*de sea!

12) *P*uffs, *p*owders, *p*atches, *bi*bles, *bi*llet-doux. (Pope)
13) *F*ull *f*athom *f*ive thy *f*ather lies. (Shakespeare)
14) A *str*ong man *str*uggling with the *sto*rms of fate.

(30) **Onomatopoeia:** It is a figure in which the sounds of words echo their sense *(i.e., the meaning of the word is suggested by the sound of similar words);* as,

1) *"Swallows <u>twittering</u> in the sky."* — in the line we get a word *'twittering'*, the sound of which echoes the sense of *'chirping birds'*, i.e., similar sound of other word reflects the meaning of actual word.

2) *'With heavy <u>**thump**</u>, a lifeless <u>**lump**</u>*
    *They <u>**dropped**</u> down one by one.'* (Coleridge)

In the lines, we get an instance of Onomatopoeia, for here the words *'thump', 'lump', 'dropped'* —<u>*reflect the sense of falling of heavy things* </u>(in the poem of 'Ancient Mariner', it means *'dead bodies'*).

It should be noted **alliteration** and **onomatopoeia** frequently go together as in the above line. **Euphemism** is also present in the last line where *a harsh truth 'dead' is said amiably* **'they dropped down one by one.'**

The Chief Characteristic:

a. <u>Sound of words</u> reflect (imitate/communicate) the sense of other words. The sound echoes a feeling or an idea.

More examples of Onomatopoeia:

3) 'It cracked and growled and roared and howled / Like noises in a sound.' (Coleridge)
   - ➤ This is an onomatopoeia. In this figure, the sounds of words — 'crackled', 'growled', 'roared' and 'howled'—echo the *sense of a sharp and loud noise.*

4) 'Soft is strain when zephyr gently blows / And the smooth stream in smoother number flows.' (Pope)
   - ➤ Here the words— 'soft', 'strain', 'gently blows, 'smooth stream', 'smoother"—echo the *sense of sweetness.*

5) 'But when the loud surges lash the sounding shore, / The hoarse rough verse should like the torrent roar. *(Echoing the sense of 'harshness')*

6) 'It will flame out, like shining from shook foil.' *(Echo the sense of 'dazzling effect')*

7) 'Generations have trod, have trod, have trod.' *(The sense of 'weariness')*

8) 'And the muttering grew to grumbling / And the grumbling grew to a mighty rumbling / And out of the houses rats came tumbling.' *(Sense of 'confusion')*

9) 'Most weary seemed the sea; weary the oar, / Weary the wandering fields of barren foam.' *(Echo the sense of 'tiredness')*

10) 'Up the high hill he heaves a huge round stone.' *(The sequence of words echoes the sense of 'labored movement')*

Pun or Paronomasia

(31) **Pun or Paronomasia:** It is a figure which '*rests on a duplicity of sense under unity of sound* (<u>has double sense or meaning of a word</u> or <u>words of similar sound</u>). Pun is also known as *Equivoque.*

1) "An ambassador is an honest man who **lies** abroad for the good of his country." — It is an example of Pun. Here, the word 'lies' has two meanings— (a) resides abroad, & (b) tells a lie. Here, a single word is used in two senses.

2) "Not on thy **sole** but on thy **soul**" — Here in the sentence we notice another variety of Pun. It has two words of similar sound which have two different spellings and different meanings. While the first word 'sole' means 'under surface of a foot', the other word 'soul' means 'spirit'.

3) "So is the **will** of a living daughter curbed by the **will** of a dead father." — Here two words-'will' & 'will' have the same sound, same spellings but two different meanings or senses— (a) one means 'desire', (b) while other means 'the legal document'.

The Chief Characteristics:
a. One word is used in two different senses,
b. Two words having same sound, but identical or dissimilar spellings with two different meanings,
c.   The figure is generally used to excite laughter, and often too seriousness or deep meaning.

More examples of Pun or Paronomasia:

4) When the piece of meat fell in the river, the dog looked at it **fondly**.
➤ This is a Pun. In this figure the duplicity of sense is expressed through the unity of sound. Here a single word, 'fondly' is used in two senses: (a) affectionately & (b) foolishly.

5) For a foolish sportsman it is easier to **follow** a hound than to **follow** an argument.
➤ This is also a Pun. Here two words—'follow' and 'follow'—having identical sound and spelling but have two different meanings: (a) to chase & (b) to understand.

6) Is life worth living? —it depends on the **liver**. [(a) human organ & (b) living person]

7) They went and **told** (i.e., reported) the sexton, and sexton **toll'd** (i.e., sounded) the bell. (Hood)

8) Would that its tone could **reach** (i.e., arrive at) the **Rich** (i.e., the wealthy men). (Hood).

9) But a cannon ball took off his legs / So he laid down his ***arms***. [the word 'arms' echo both (a) limbs & (b) weapons]

10) Though he is a professor his knowledge on **sound** is not **sound**. [(a) branch of study & (b) deep]

11) _She is too ***light*** to bear this ***light***. [(a) frivolous & (b) illumination]

12) What he hit is history and what he missed is mystery. [(a) his story & (b) my story]

13) If a woman loses her husband, she pines for a ***second***. [(a) a second's time & (b) a second husband]

14) The man cares for the ***pages*** of his house but not for the ***pages*** of a single book. [(a) servants & (b) printed leaves]

15) O world! Thou wast the forest to this ***hart***. [(a) red deer & (b) heart]

16) At my death ***Thy Son*** Hall shine as he shines now. [(a) Son of God & (b) the Sun]

17) For if the Jew do cut but deep enough, / I'll pay it with all my ***heart***. [(a) suffer in the heart & (seek revenge fully]

18) I've met with many a breeze before, / But never such a ***blow***. [(a) stroke & (b) blowing of wind]

7. Figures based on Construction

When words are placed in their normal order, as we studied so far in English Grammar, they are able to communicate a sense or a thought, what we generally use in our normal communication in speaking or writing, is called a common place language. They are used to provide information, asking, giving order, advice, etc.

Poets, writers, or orators—are not happy always with this common place language and they often slightly do change the position of normal word-order (usual construction of sentences) to make their expression highly impressive and much more effective, and this they do by different

<u>means</u>. These means are known as figures based on Construction, beside the others (other figures).

In this class of rhetoric, there are the highest number of figures which are set from sl. No- 32 to 50. The list is given below:
32) Interrogation or Rhetorical Question, 33) Exclamation, 34) Hyperbaton or Anastrophe, 35) Prolepsis (Anticipation), 36) Chiasmus or Inversion, 37) Hendiadys, 38) Tautology, 39) Pleonasm, 40) Ellipsis, 41) Asyndeton, 42) Polysyndeton, 43) Anaphora, 44) Epistrophe, 45) Anadiplosis, 46) Epanadiplosis, 47) Palilogy, 48) Catachresis, 49) Anacoluthon, 50) Aposiopesis

Rhetorical Question, Exclamation,

(32) **Interrogation:** It is a figure in which something is strongly affirmed or denied in the form of a question. It is also known as *Erotesis* or ***Rhetorical Question.***

Interpretation: Normally we use interrogation to ask question in order to know something, we want an answer; but *in rhetorical question, interrogation is used not to ask, but to affirm or deny something effectively*. In the words of Fowler, it is 'a more striking substitute for a statement.'

In Rhetorical question, the answer is always implied in the question itself. It does not intend to get an answer to know anything different, but to say something effectively and emphatically as an assertive statement. If the question is in the affirmative, a strong denial is intended. Thus, in the examples:
1) 'Am I my brother's keeper?'
2) 'Can a leopard change its spots?'
Their answers are an emphatic 'No'.

If the question is in the negative, a strong affirmation is suggested; as,
3) 'If you prick us, do we not bleed?' (Shakespeare)
4) 'If you poison us, do we not die?' (Shakespeare)

> Here, the answer of each rhetorical question is an emphatic 'yes'.

The Chief Characteristics of Interrogation:
a. The sentence is found in the form of question;
b. When it is in the affirmative, a strong denial is intended.

c. When it is in the negative, a strong affirmation is suggested;
d. The answer is implied in the question itself.

More Examples

5) Am I not free to do this as I choose?
→ This is an interrogation.
→ In this figure, a strong affirmation or denial is done in the form of a question.
→ Here, in the above line, a strong 'yes' is suggested, and the answer is implied in the question itself.

6) Am I not a man and a brother?
7) Can the Ethiopian change his skin, or the leopard his spots?
8) Shall we receive good at the hand of God /And evil not receive? (Browning)
9) If you tickle us, do we not laugh? (Shakespeare)
10) For who can think submission? (Milton)
11) Who is here so vile that will not love his country? (Shakespeare)
12) Who is here so rude that would not be a Roman? (Shakespeare)
13) Who would not sing for Lycidas? (Milton)
14) But why should we care about the opinion of many?

(33) **Exclamation:** It is a figure which contains an abrupt (sudden) expression of some emotion, wish or contemplation, frequently introduced by interjections or such words as '**how**', '**what**', etc.

Hardly it has any difference with normal exclamation.

Study the examples:
1) Oh, that those lips had language! (Cowper) [wish]

2) Oh, for a draught of vintage! (Keats) [wish]

3) Had I the wings of a dove! [wish]

4) How sharper than a serpent's tooth it is / To have a thankless child! (Shakespeare) [contemplation]

5) Oh, the depth of the riches both of the wisdom and knowledge of God! [contemplation]

6) What a piece of work is a man! (Shakespeare) [emotion]

7)   But alas, Caesar must bleed for it! [emotion]

Hyperbaton or Anastrophe, Prolepsis or Anticipation

(34)   **Hyperbaton or Anastrophe:** It is a figure in which the grammatical order of words in a sentence is inverted to secure emphasis or rhetorical effect. The figure is also identified with 'Anastrophe'.
*The **inversion** or **hyperbaton** or **anastrophe** happens often in poems; as in poems of Keats:*

1)   "Much have I travelled in the realms of gold" —we get an example of Hyperbaton, for the normal order of words— *'I have travelled much in the realms of gold'.*

*This inversion is not bound with any particular Part of Speech **but may be with any one or ones.***

2)   *Just* are the ways of God. [***in place of:*** The ways of God are just.]

3)   *Smooth runs* the water where the brook is deep. (Shakespeare) [***in place of:*** The water runs smooth...]

4)   *Out of evil cometh* good. [***in place of:*** Good cometh out of evil.]

5)   A woman *moved* is like a fountain *troubled*. (Milton) [***in place of:*** A moved woman is like a troubled fountain.]

6)   *Me* he restored and *him* he hanged. [***in place of:*** He restored me and he hanged him.]

7)   No more battle's sound /Was heard the world around. [***in place of:*** /Was heard around the world]

8)   Yet I'll not shed her blood, / Nor scar that whiter skin of hers than snow. (Shakespeare) [/**N**or scar that skin of hers whiter than snow]

9)   Thrice is he armed that hath his quarrel just. (Shakespeare) [He is armed thrice ...]

10) Round many western islands have I been. (Keats) [I have been rounding many western islands.]

11) Most blameless is he. (Tennyson) [He is most blameless]

12) My days among the dead are past. (Southey) [My days are past among the dead.]

13) Out of the suffering comes the serious mind. (Ruskin) [The serious mind comes out of the suffering]

14) Sweet are the uses of adversity. (Shakespeare) [The uses of adversity are sweet.]

(35)   **Prolepsis or Anticipation:** It is a figure in which a descriptive term (*an adjective or a participle*) is used before it is strictly applicable to represent some event which is yet to occur, but presented as having already happened; as,

So, it is about the anticipatory use of an epithet before its time to come;
as,

1) 'Fill *full* the cup.' —*the epithet 'full' is used when still the process of filling is on or not completed*; but the listener gets the impression well what the speaker intends.
   It may slightly seem to be like a **Vision** *(seeing past event or an event of anticipated future)* or a **Transferred Epithet,** or so called **'Hypallage'** *(shifted of participle or an adjective from its proper object to another which is mentally related or associated)*; but it is different from them too.

Study the examples:
2) 'For me the *widow*'s mate expires.' [being '**widow**' is the condition to come after one's mate or husband expires, but before that, the epithet has been used for the 'woman'.]
3) 'They shot him *dead*.' [here the man is presumed to be **dead** being shot before he really dies. However, if it was written, '*He was shot to death*', it would not be a prolepsis or anticipation but a common language statement.]

Chiasmus (or Inversion), & Hendiadys

(36)   **Chiasmus:** It is a figure in which *the order of words* in the first part (main words) *are reversed* in the second part of a sentence *for sake of emphasis or poetic effect.* Thus, the inversion may produce two different ideas in the sentence, though not always; as,

1) 'Live to learn, learn to live'
   —It is an example of Chiasmus.

➢ The words in the first part (i.e., *'Live to learn'*) are reversed in the second part *('learn to live')* and they build two different meanings or sense, and it draws our attention to the contrast.

   (It reminds us of Antithesis in which two contrasted ideas are set in two parts of the sentence; as, 'United we stand, divided we fall' to give emphasis on a particular idea. Here, it is about the 'Strength of Unity')

➢ In Chiasmus, the inversion happens to the order of words, in the arrangement of words and may produce two different ideas, not opposite. In Antithesis, two opposite ideas are compulsory, and they are set side by side in two parts of the same sentence.

➢ Let's play a game. Choose one:

→ Why do we **live for**? —to learn?

→ Why do we **learn for**? —to live?

2) 'Eat to live, or live to eat' —what should we choose between them for a man? [*'Eat to live, not live to eat'*—should be your answer, must Peter think for a man. However, you may express another.]

3) 'Fair is foul and foul is fair.' —what is fair is foul to the three witches in Macbeth of Shakespeare, and what is foul (to human beings) is fair to them. The order of words is repeated in the second part, and we have two ideas. Thus, it is an example of Chiasmus.

4) *'Beauty is truth, truth beauty.'* (Keats) [Truth and beauty are emphasized to be identical.]

5) He was *a rake among scholars* and *a scholar among rakes.* (Macaulay) [two contrasted ideas are expressed by the inversion of the order of words.]

6) May you *stand long* and *long stand* terror the tyrants. (Byron) [Order of words are inversed and two succeeding probabilities are expressed. In the second part, Hyperbaton also occurs.]

7) For *sand and dune*, and *dune and sand*/ Are all that I go by. [similar idea is expressed through the inversion of order of words.]

8) For *the sky and the sea,* and *the sea and the sky*/ Lay like a load on my weary eye. (Coleridge) [it emphasizes an idea, besides producing the rhythmic effect.]

9) So, *these were wed,* and *merrily rang the bell,* /*Merrily rang the bells,* and *these were wed.* (Tennyson) [Chiasmus occurs along with Prolepsis & also Hyperbaton with the word, 'merrily'.]

10) And *singing* still dost *soar,* and *soaring* ever *singest.* (Shelley) [to emphasize the two actions are happening simultaneously.]

Distinction among: Antithesis, Hyperbaton & Chiasmus: -

✓ **Inversion** occurs in three of them.

    ✓ However, *inversion of grammatical order of words occurs in* **Hyperbaton**; *as in,* 'Just are the ways of God' *in place of*: **The ways of God are just.** There is no repetition of words in Hyperbaton.

✓ **In Chiasmus,** the order of words in the first part is repeated or inversed in the second part of the sentence, and often to mean two different things, beside producing rhythmic effect in the lines; as in, 'Fair is foul, foul is fair'. However, this may sometimes, reflects same idea; as in, 'Beauty is truth, truth beauty.'

✓ On the other hand, **in Antithesis**, there are always contrasted ideas set side by side in a balance form to emphasis an idea that comes from the both; as in 'United we stand, divided we fall'— two contrasted ideas are set in the balance form to emphasis the idea, of 'the strength of unity'. Both parts of the sentence contribute to the formation of singular idea to make it stronger and more forceful.

(37) **Hendiadys:** It is a figure in which a complex idea is expressed by two Nouns joined by 'and', where one Noun acts of an Adjective to the other Noun; as,

1) The hall was full of melody and misses.
➢ This is a Hendiadys. A complex idea is expressed by two Noun, joined by 'and' and one Noun performs the function of an adjective. Here 'melody' and 'misses' are used to express *'melodious misses.*

2) They poured drinks in *goblet* & *gold*. [i.e., golden goblets]
3) His look drew *audience* and *attention*. [i.e., attentive audience]

4) The air is resonant with *joy* and *song*. [i.e., joyous songs]
5) Our *yoke* and *sufferance* show us womanish. [i.e., suffering yoke]
6) *Mysteries* and *presences* innumerable. [i.e., mysterious presences]
7) *Perfume* and *flowers* fell in showers. [i.e., perfumed flowers]
8) That life is lost to *love* and *me*. [i.e., lovelorn me]
9) It stood in *darkness* and in the *shadow* of death. [i.e., dark shadow]
10) The *trade* and *profit* of the nations. [i.e., profitable trade]
11) The gentle tale of *love* and *languishment*. [i.e., languishing love]
12) *Joy* and *tidings*. [i.e., joyous tidings]

Tautology, Pleonasm, Ellipsis, & Asyndeton,

(38) **Tautology & its variation:** It is a figure [the term 'tautology' means 'saying the same thing'] in which superfluous synonyms (of words or a phrase) are placed side by side; as,

1) 'The very *scheme* and *plan* of his life failed on account of the non-co-operation of his wife'.

➤ This is a Tautology. In this figure, superfluous synonyms are placed side by side in the same sentence, when either one of which would have served the purpose well.

➤ **Read other examples:**

2) My friend spoke *all at once together*.
3) It is a proposal *intolerable, not to be endured*.
4) Unfortunately, he did not confine his remarks to *only one* subject.
5) The woman was quite *exhausted* and *fatigued*.
6) The Constitution places women on the *same equality* with men.
7) He has at last become *poor, pauper* and *beggar* by ill luck.
8) It is a *false lie*.
9) The activities of this club are not *limited only* to swimmers and bathers.
10) Few can hear the *noiseless inaudible* foot of time.
11) The king was noted for his *bounty* and *benevolence.*
12) She danced for one full hour in *joy* and *delight*.
13) He wishes her *happiness* and *felicity*.
14) The army delighted at the *glitter of arms* and the *flash of weapons*.
15) The students arrived *one after another in succession*.
16) He was able to preserve his *peace* and *equanimity*.
17) Thou wast *not born for death, immortal* Bird! (Keats)

And like many more; as,

<table>
<tr><td>• Well and good</td><td>• Hale and hearty</td><td>• Kith and kin</td></tr>
<tr><td>• Bag and baggage</td><td>• House and home</td><td>• Time and tide</td></tr>
<tr><td>• First and foremost</td><td>• Lord and master</td><td>• Pure and simple</td></tr>
<tr><td>• save and except</td><td>• Null & void</td><td>• Leaps and bounds</td></tr>
<tr><td>• Trade and commerce</td><td>• Common and vulgar</td><td>• Sum and substance</td></tr>
<tr><td>• Separate and distinct</td><td>• Final and unalterable</td><td>• Privation and want.</td></tr>
</table>

(39)   **Pleonasm:** Pleonasm is almost similar to 'Tautology' in terms of _using 'unnecessary additional words'_ in a sentence. In this sense, you may term Pleonasm as a kind of variation of 'Tautology.

However, in **_Tautology_** the unnecessary words are the synonyms, in **_Pleonasm_** the words are not directly synonyms.

So, Pleonasm is a figure in which some unnecessary additional words are used in the same sentence which are not directly synonyms:

Note: Tautology and Pleonasm—may be regarded as the grammatical errors, but its popularity among the poets and writers- has given them the status of rhetoric figures, and thus there are many others.

a) '**_I saw_** it with my **_own eyes_**.'
➢ This is a Pleonasm. When the idea might have been well expressed by simply **_'I saw it'_**, some words are added to it additionally— **_'with my own eyes'_**. It not only made the sentence lengthy, but also made the sense of the sentence emphatic & clearer.

b) The object has no _intrinsic_ value _in itself_.
c) I _eyed_ him with a _look_ of contempt.
d) Her mind was _full_ of _great many_ ideas.
e) The _heavens above_ and the _earth beneath_ frowned at the sinner.
f) _I wrote_ the document _with my own hands_.
g) They _returned back again_ to the same town _from whence they came from_.
h) I shall not _prejudge_ the verdict _in advance_.

(40)   **Ellipsis:** It is a figure in which a word or words are omitted for sake of compactness, brevity, elegance, or emphasis; as,

[It is the opposite term of earlier two, Tautology or Pleonasm.]

a) 'Elizabeth and Leicester [were] / Beating oars. (T. S. Eliot)
b) To the [this is] no reason.
c) The woman talks all the way [as she goes] upstairs to [pay] a visit.
d) The gangster was hanged and his helpers [were] mercilessly beaten.
e) The harm done by wine is greater than [that done by] tea.

(41)   **Asyndeton:** It is a figure in which conjunctions are omitted for vividness, energy, liveliness, or effect; as,

a) Simple, erect, severe, austere, [and] sublime.
b) I came, I saw, I conquered.
c) I slip, I slide, I gleam, I dance. (Tennyson)
d) Theirs be the music, the colour, the glory, the gold. (Masefield)
e) From art more various are the blessings sent /Wealth, commerce, honour, liberty, content. (Goldsmith)
f) The spring, the head, the fountain of your blood/Is stopped. (Shakespeare).

On your mark, get, set, go!

Polysyndeton, Anaphora, Epistrophe,

(42)   **Polysyndeton:** [It is the opposite term of Asyndeton.] Polysyndeton is a figure in which conjunctions are repeated with an artistic sense to emphasize each particular idea; as,

a) Contented toil, and hospitable care,
   And kind connubial tenderness are there,
   And piety with wishes placed above,
   And steady loyalty, and faithful love. (Goldsmith)

b) Envy and calumny and hate and pain. (Shelley)

c) Thrice to thine and thrice to mine,
   And thrice again to make up nine. (Shakespeare)

d) Most men eddy about

Here and there—eat *and* drink,
Scatter *and* love *and* hate,
Gather *and* squander. (Arnold)

e) Neither blindness, *nor* gout, *nor* age, *nor* penury, *nor* domestic afflictions, *nor* political disappointments, *nor* abuse, *nor* proscription, *nor* neglect had a power to disturb his sedate and majestic patience. (Macaulay)

(43) **Anaphora/ Epanaphora:** It is a figure in which same expression is repeated at the beginning of several successive clauses, sentence, for sake of producing melody, mostly in poetic lines; as,

a) *Theirs* not to make reply,
Theirs not to reason why,
Theirs but to do and die. **(Tennyson)**

b) *What I* spent I had
What I kept I lost,
What I gave I have.

c) *Ring out* old shapes of foul disease,
Ring out the narrowing lust of gold;
Ring out the thousand wars of old,
Ring in the thousand years of peace.
(Tennyson)

d) *There is* a pleasure on a pathless woods,
There is a rapture on the lonely shore,
There is society where none intrudes. **(Byron)**

(44) **Epistrophe:** [This figure is the opposite of Anaphora in relating the place of repeated words in the lines. This figure is also known as **Antistrophe** or **Epiphora**] It is a figure in which each **clause** or **sentence** ends with the same word or phrase, for the energy to the language; as,

a) We were born to *sorrow*, pass our time in *sorrow*, end our time in *sorrow*.
b) The teachers are *wrong*; philosophers are *wrong*; scientists are *wrong*; sages are *wrong*; all are *wrong* except you. **(P. to his spouse)**

c) Reading maketh a full _man_, conference a ready _man_, and writing an exact _man_. **(Bacon)**
d) The storm may _enter_, the rain may _enter_, but the king of England cannot _enter_. **(Pitt)**
e) Smoking is bad for _health_; drinking is bad for _health_; over-eating is bad for _health_; there is meditation is the only wealth and not bad for _health_. **(P. to his disciple)**
f) I have said _it_; I repeat _it_; I will swear to _it_.

Anadiplosis, Epanadiplosis, Palilogy

(45) **Epanastrophe or Anadiplosis:** [This figure is a variation of **Epistrophe** or the combination of both **Epistrophe** & **Anaphora,** when Anaphora & Epistrophe are opposite to each other]
Epanastrophe or Anadiplosis is a figure in which _the ending of a sentence_, i.e., phrase, clause or line _is repeated_ and emphasized _at the beginning of the next_; as,
a) O stealing time, the subject of _delay_,
   Delay the rack of unrefrain'd desire.

   b) You must wake and _call me early_,
      Call me early, mother dear. **(Tennyson)**

c) Tomorrow'll be the happiest time _of all the glad New Year._
      Of all the glad New year, mother, the maddest, merriest day.
      (Tennyson)

(46) **Epanadiplosis:** [This figure is a variation of **Epanastrophe** or **Anadiplosis**]
   Epanadiplosis is a figure in which a sentence begins and ends with the same word; as,
a) _The thoughts_ are but over flowing of the mind, and the tongue is but a servant of _the thoughts_. **(Sidney)**

   b) _Sweet_ is the breath of morn, her rising _sweet_. **(Milton)**

c) _Moor_ and stubble and mist, stubble and mist and _moor_.
   ❑   *Note: Epanados, Epanalepsis, Epanorthosis*—are the variations of '*Epanadiplosis.*

(47)   **Palilogy**: It is a figure in which a word or phrase is repeated for sake of emphasis.

a)   *Happy, happy* boughs! That cannot shed. (Keats)

  b)   *Alas alas on on the skull the skull the skull the skull* in Connemara. (Becket)

   c)   *O no*, *he cannot* be *good,* that *know not* why he is *good*, but stands *so far good*, as his fortune may keep him unassailed. (Sidney)

d)   *O earth, O earth, O earth*, hear the voice of the dead.

Catachresis, Anacoluthon, Aposiopesis

(48)   **Catachresis:** Some popular misuses of words (particularly adjectives) to the nouns, are known as the figure of Catachresis.

a)   *Blind* mouths! That scarce themselves know how to hold / A sheep-hook. (Milton) *[blind i.e., greedy as to be careless of spiritual attainments]*

b)   She possessed a *beautiful* voice. *[beautiful voice i.e., sweet voice]*

c)   She wore a *nice* dress on that occasion. *[nice i.e., fine]*

(49)   **Anacoluthon:** The use of broken sentence construction which lacks the grammatical sequence of words.
When a sentence is started in one way, continued and finished in another way —is known as Anacoluthon. Anacoluthon or the violation of sequence occurs under strong emotion or energy of the speaker.

a)   Why do I trifle thus with his despair / Is done to cure it? (Shakespeare)

b)   His young and open soul—dissimulation / Is foreign to him. (Coleridge)

(50)   **Aposiopesis:** It is a figure in which a writer or speaker breaks off suddenly leaving the sentence unfinished for the sake of effect.
Thus, is done, for the speaker or writer assumes that his suppressed sentiment or statement will be understood and supplied with suitable word or words by the hearers or readers by themselves; as,

a)   I will have such revenges on you both,
     That all the world shall— (Shakespeare)

    b)   If we should fail—
    c)   You know what I—but let's forget it!

        d)   And yet methinks I see in thy face,
        What thou shouldst be— (Shakespeare)

Section-B. Prosody (the Grammar of Verse)

The term **'Prosody'** *(from Latin **'Prosodia'**, meaning <u>the accent of syllable</u>, & from Greek **'Prosoidia'**, meaning <u>a song sung to music'</u>)—* **is the study of the constitution of Verse.**

<u>The term 'Prosody'</u> is chiefly concerned with *rhythm, metre, rhyme* and *stanza forms of a verse or poem.* Thus, prosody deals with the laws which govern the structure of a verse, so as of a poem and poetry.

Both prose and verse have to observe the rule of grammar. *Verse, in addition to the above, pays attention to **metre, rhyme**, and **regularity of pauses (rhythm)** <u>which constitute the harmony and melody of verse</u>, from which a prose is free and different from the verse.* So, Prosody is concerned with these pleasing qualities of verse.

In spite of all these, a poetry is not opposed to a prose. A prose may also be poetic and a poetry without metre, rhyme, and regularity of pauses (rhythm) may be regarded a prosaic poem. And both are two different and independent genres of literature.

science and poetry: Poetry being an art is opposed to science. The chief aim of science is to impart knowledge, and that of poetry is to give pleasure. The pleasure of poetry rests both on **matter** & **manner** – on the thoughts (subject matter) and the ways they are expressed (manner).

Prosody deals with not with thought or subject matter but with the manner or form, how or in what way the thoughts of poetry expressed. Thus, prosody treats with the rules that regulate poetic composition. It does not relate to or governs on subject matter or thoughts of poets or composers.

When we use the words— **poetry, poem** and **verse** — we mean the same thing '<u>a metrical composition</u>', though difference lies in them in length and meters.

<u>Let's discuss</u>, where do they similar, and where lies any difference. ***Poetry***, as per Oxford Advanced Learner's Dictionary, is a <u>collection of poems</u>, or <u>poems in general</u>. So, it is a plural number according to this sense, 'a book of poetry' means 'a book containing a collection of poems. When poem may be singular and plural—poem & poems; poetry is always plural number 'poems in general' or 'a collection of poems'.

A ***poem*** *means* 'a piece of writing' *<u>in which the words are chosen for their effective sound </u>*and to *<u>represent images the poet intends to deliver</u>* or *<u>create by the color of his imagination</u>*, *<u>emotions</u>*, i<u>ntellectuals</u>, etc. The words which are used in a poem may have double meanings, literal and suggestive. The words are arranged in ***<u>separate lines</u>***, <u>usually</u> with ***<u>repeated rhythm</u>***, and <u>often the **lines rhyme at the end**</u>. The lines of a poem, as well as of a verse are again divided in **foot, pause,** and **metre.**

A verse, *in its widest sense, is* 'any metrical composition' *that also means for a poem. In earlier times plays written in 'metrical lines'; and thus they; a poem, a verse or a play differ themselves from a prose. However, a verse, in its narrowest sense, merely means* 'a metrical line or two, or a unit of lines, or even a stanza, as a unit or a part of a poem or a song.' And Prosody is the study of such a metrical composition that may be of a line, two or more, of a stanza or a poem. A verse consists in lines in regular rhythm or pattern, generally end in rhyme.

Alexander Poe, so why, has defined poetry as 'rhythmical creation of beauty', *and according to* ***Watts-Dunton*** 'poetry seems to require not only intellectual life and emotional life but also rhythmical life'. In ordinary usage too, poetry is both *imaginative* and *metrical*. But poetry often exists without rhyme; it may exist without regular metre, as a poetry free verse.

A prosody is the study of a line or a verse, i.e., that may be of a line, two or more, a stanza or a poem. It is the grammar which deals with metrical lines, about its 'syllables' accented or unaccented, 'feet', 'metre', 'pause' and also about rhymes.

A poetic line or a verse is generally 'a kind of metrical composition' that means it is made up of a number of feet or a series of rhythmical *syllables, accented or unaccented, have pause and produce rhythms and has rhymes too.*

In the above said words, lies the <u>subject matter of the</u> '**Prosody'**. *A prosody is to know or study the constitution of Verse. So, Prosody, is rightly said as the 'grammar of verse'.* If we study Prosody, we'll come to know of different syllables of a poetic line, i.e., of a verse, accented, unaccented, foot, pause and metre, rhyme and about regular or irregular rhythm, maintained in the arrangement of lines. Regarding this, '***Scansion'*** is also an important term to discuss.

Syllables types: Accented or Unaccented

Syllable: A syllable is *a unit of pronunciation.* It is a *sound or a combination of sounds produced at a single impulse of the voice.* In practical application *'a syllable refers to a word or a part of a word uttered by a single effort of the voice.'*
Its utterance is of course done by the vocal organs with a single push of air-pressure from the lungs. However, in writing, syllables are divided by a hyphen (-), the punctuation mark. So, scansion in prosody is not possible without sound conception of the syllable.

Note the following features:
a. A syllable usually contains only one vowel sound, no matter how many vowels may go with it, thus the words like, ***goal, head*** & ***tooth***—have more than one vowel but they have only one vowel sound in them.
b. A syllabic consonant or a sonorant is capable of forming a complete syllable without a vowel, as '**l**' in *a-ble, mid-dle, hum-ble*; '**m**' in *bot-tom*; '**n**' in *but-ton, sud-den* & '**r**' in *cen-tre, me-tre,* etc.

A word <u>having one unit of sound</u> is called a **monosyllabic** word, and that <u>having several units of sound</u>, especially more than three, is known as a '**Polysyllabic word'**. However, we'll try to name particular name for per one as far we can:

Name of Words	*Examples*
Monosyllabic words:	Book, shoe, cat, bat, man, pan, etc.
Disyllabic words	<u>Fa-ther</u>, <u>mo-ther</u>, <u>bro-ther</u>, <u>sis-ter</u>, etc.

Tri-syllabic words	<u>Hand-ker-chief</u>, <u>coun-ta-ble</u>, <u>beau-ti-ful,</u>
Tetra-syllabic words	Un-coun-ta-ble/ in-di-vi-dual, im-po-si-ble,
Penta-syllabic words	Te-tra-sy-lla-ble/ pen-ta-sy-lla-bic
Hexta-syllabic words	In-com-pre-hen-si-ble/an-te-di-lu-vi-an
Hepta-syllabic words	U-ti-li-ta-ri-a-nism/a-ca-ro-do-ma-ti-a
Octa-syllabic words	A-mi-no-a-ci-du-ri-a/in-tel-lec-tu-a-li-za-tion
Nobum-syllabic words	Ab-do-mi-no-hys-te-ro-to-my/hy-per-cho-les-te-ro-le-mi-a
Deca-syllabic words	He-te-ro-phe-no-me-no-lo-gi-cal / dii-o-do-hy-dro-xy-qui-no-li-ne

Syllables— accented & unaccented:

Syllable are of two kinds—<u>open</u> and <u>closed</u>. *An open syllable is one <u>ending in a vowel</u>*; as the first syllable of **'si-lent'**. *A closed syllable is one <u>ending in a consonant</u>*; as the first and third syllables of **'cat-a-pult'**.

There is a controversy in respect of syllabification. For example, 'even' is syllabified as either *'e-ven'* or *'ev-en'* and 'anklet' as either *'ank-let'* or *'an-klet'*. And it is due to the different pronunciation pattern throughout different countries and tend predominant in different centuries. However, I am here, will try to give which is popular, at present, and to us.

As said, **syllables may be unaccented** (go, catch, sad, trek, man, all) **or accented** (a′llow′ed, ye′t, sti′ll, de′-cent, fra-te′r-nal, pho-to-gra′ph-ic), etc. (the sign (′) is used to show the accented syllable) As a rule, a monosyllable (e.g., *man)* has no accent, but it takes often and a <u>monosyllabic proper noun take one always</u>; and which has accent, has its own rhythm too. Generally, disyllables (hu′-man, re′-al), trisyllables (di-me′n-*sion, fore-or-dai′n*), polly syllables (*hu-ma′n-i-ty, re-a′l-i-ty*) have accented syllables and they have their own rhythms too.

Stress, Emphasis, & Accent

Stress: *Stress is 'a strong or special exertion of the voice on a word, or on a part of a word, so as to distinguish it from another.'* It is a generic name applying to both *emphasis* and *accent* which are *two special types of stress* and which are the effect of loudness which helps to produce distinctness.

Emphasis: *Emphasis is the stress or loudness of voice deliberately thrown upon an entire word to distinguish it from another*, as in '*Him I* like, her *I* hate' or in '*I* love him' or 'His parents are poor but *honest*'. This emphasis does not have any particular rule. It is mainly or may be said entirely, depends on the speaker, based on his intention, though there is some about the accent on the words; and there too, have differences through different nations and upon their manner of pronunciation. The main thing is rhythm, how the provider or creator, speaker or artist will lead them. Shifting of emphasis or stress has different shades of meanings.

Accent: Whereas, the accent is also a kind of stress or loudness of voice thrown upon a single syllable. *It helps the particular syllable to stand out from the other syllables of the same word and to make it more prominent than the rest* in respect of distinctness of pronunciation. The strongly stressed syllables are known as accented syllables and are marked by (') accent sign. Those syllables which receive no stress are known as unaccented syllables, and they bear either no sign or that given in bracket (∪ or ×)

The accents of words are not strictly fixed. It may be different through nations and time to time, from ancient to modern. Despite this inconsistency here it is an attempt to find certain regular features about accentuation of English words as per British and Indian. The following examples will show which syllables are accented and which are not. Here the sign (') is used to show the accented syllable and for unaccented I have not used any sign:

- 'Do′ you wi′sh the world were be′t-ter?'
- E′duca′tion, re′cog′nize, re′cti′fy,
- begi′n, fla′p-per; a′f-ter, a-bou′t, af-ter-noo′n
- I′n a | ba′t-tle; I′n a | ma′ze / lo′st I | ga′ze
- My hai′r| is gre′y | but not |with yea′rs.

Importance of Accent: Accent is akin to Latin **'ictus'**, a blow, and signifies that a particular syllable is to receive a blow by which it is rendered prominent and loud. Hence it denotes the sharpness of the stroke.

The sound pattern caused by the accented and unaccented syllables produces the **rhythm of a speech** or **a line**, and when this sound pattern is regular, recurrent and measurable into smaller equal time-taking units (called the 'feet'), we get a line consists of such feet, two or three, is known as 'metre'.

*Accent is, thus, responsible for both **rhythm** and **metre** of verse. That is why '**accent**' is rightly considered as the guiding principle of English Prosody.*

Rhythm, Feet, Metre & Classification

Rhythm: The term 'Rhythm' comes from the Greek word 'rhuthmos', meaning 'measured motion or flow'. It is the basic principle of the spoken language, whether prose or verse. The term '**Rhythm**' may be described as *'the sound pattern made by the rise and fall of the stress in speech'*.

Foot: 'Feet' is the plural number of 'foot'. In prose this sound pattern (the fall of stress) which governs 'rhythm' of speech, may or may not be regular, but in poetry or verse, this sound pattern (the fall of stress) is so regular that it is possible to divide a poetic line into a number of recurrent, equal time-taking units. Each unit is known as *'**foot**'* and the units together of a line are called *'**feet**'; as,*

'The cu'r-| few to'lls | the kne'll | of pa'rt- |ing da'y'.

> Here we observe not only equal time-intervals between the accented syllables but also a *regular* arrangement of accented and unaccented syllables which constitute a peculiar musical tone or sound of the verse. Thus, in the above line, there are five feet (pl of foot), and the line is known as 'pentameter' (a metrical line of five feet).

Metre: The term *'Metre'* comes from the Greek word 'metron' meaning *'measure'*. So, Metre is the measurement of units (the recurrent and equal time-taking units). So, in a sense, and true sense, a meter is nothing but a collection of feet (pl of foot). Each unit (recurrent and equal time-taking unit of accented or unaccented syllables, is known as foot, more than one foot is known as feet, and the poetic line, consists of such regular sound pattern or feet, is known as 'meter'; and the regular sound pattern of rise and fall of the voice, due to accented and unaccented syllables, is termed as 'Rhythm' (it includes accents and pause of a line).

❑ Study the <u>Distinction between 'Rhythm' & 'Metre'</u>

Rhythm	Metre
1. Rhythm is an infinitely varying movement.	1. Metre is a definite & fixed pattern.
2. *It is a flow*, that'll go on with accented and unaccented syllables.	2. Metre is *a measurement of feet* in a line (a foot consists of two to three syllables, neither less nor more) which is fixed to work on after the end of the line.
3. It *implies the wave like rise and fall of our voice* which is *determined by accented and unaccented syllables* in words of a line or a sentence.	3. Metre implies *the division* of that voice (*of a line) into similar units* having standard features.
4. Rhythm is *applied to both prose and poetry*.	4. Metre, as denotes a **measured rhythm**, *is précised to poetry only*.

Classification of Feet & Metre:

As said each metrical line of a verse is divided into similar units or groups of syllables and each unit of which is called a **Foot** (or **Measure**).

Now, the question is, *how many syllable are there* (what is the maximum number of syllables in a foot?)

It is said, it (the number of syllables) may be either two or three, but it cannot be less than two or more than three.

And base on this (according to the number of syllables that can *exist in a foot*) **English feet are of two kinds**, (and each of which has their sub-divisions):

A. **Disyllabic Foot**, that consists of two syllables (i.e., one foot that has two syllables); and

B. **Tri-syllabic Foot** that consists of three syllables (i.e., one foot that has three syllables in it).

However, according to the character & number of syllables, accented and unaccented, the **English Feet of Prosody** are **chiefly of five kinds**; and including two rare feet of two syllables, the number is **seven**:

A. **Disyllabic Foot**, that consists of two syllables; and it has _two and rarely two (2+2)_, total four variations or sub-divisions:
  1. **Iamb (Iambus):** in which an unaccented is followed by an accented syllable.   [× ′ | × ′ | × ′]
  2. **Trochee:** in which an accented is followed by an unaccented syllable.   [′ × | ′ × | ′ ×]
  3. **A Spondee:** in which both syllables are accented. [′ ′ | ′ ′ | ′ ′]
  4. **Pyrrhic:** in which both syllables are unaccented. [× × | × × | × ×]

B. **Tri-syllabic Foot** that consists of three syllables, and it has three variations cum sub-divisions:
  5. **Anapaest:** in which two unaccented syllables are followed by an accented syllable. [× × ′ | × × ′ | × × ′]
  6. **Dactyl:** in which an accented syllable is followed by two unaccented syllables.   [′ × × | ′ × × | ′ × ×]
  7. **Amphibrach:** in which an accented syllable is placed between two unaccented syllables. [× ′ × | × ′ × | × ′ ×]

Though there is a fixed rule about the number of syllables in a foot, there is no such one regarding the number of feet in a metrical line. **English metre**, so, may be various according to the number feet in a line and they **are of eight kinds:** monometer, dimeter, trimeter, tetrameter, pentameter, hexameter, heptameter, octameter.
So, theoretically speaking, there can be forty type of meters (5 × 8 or 7× 8) or fifty-six types of meters in English.

Iamb, Trochee, and **Anapaest** are the commonest English feet, while Spondee, Pyrrhic, Amphibrach & Dactyl are occasional ones.
  The fundamental principle of English prosody is that there can be one and only one accented syllable in a foot (except: **Spondee** & **Pyrrhic** which are two variations of regular feet)

The sign of a feet division is a vertical line [|]. This sign is not put either at the beginning or at the end of a metrical line, but only at the point of division.

The Examples of seven feet. Carefully study them:

  1. **Iamb (Iambus):** in which an unaccented is followed by an accented syllable. [× ′ | × ′ | × ′]
     ✓   The cu ′ r |few to ′ lls | the kne ′ ll | of pa ′ rt | ing da ′ y.

2. **Trochee:** in which an accented is followed by an unaccented syllable. [′× | ′× | ′×]
   - ✓ Ho′pe is | ba′n-ished / Jo′ys are | va′n-ished.

3. **A Spondee:** in which both syllables are accented. [′′ | ′′ | ′′]
   - ✓ Ro′ck ca′ves, | La′kes, Fe′ns, | Bo′gs, De′ns | and sha′des | of dea′th. (Milton)

4. **Pyrrhic:** in which both syllables are unaccented. [× × | × × | × ×]
   - ✓ My′way | **is to** |be-gi′n |**with the** | be-gi′n |-ing.

5. **Anapaest:** in which two unaccented syllables are followed by an accented syllable. [× ×′ | × ×′ | × ×′]
   - ✓ The As-sy′r- | ian came do′wn | like a wo′lf | on the fo′ld. (Byron)

6. **Dactyl:** in which an accented syllable is followed by two unaccented syllables. [′× × | ′× × | ′ × ×]
   - ✓ Tou′ch her not | sco′rn-ful-ly, / Thi′nk of her | mou′rn-ful-ly.

7. **Amphibrach:** in which an accented syllable is placed between two unaccented syllables. [×′ × | × ′ × | × ′ ×]
   - ✓ The da′ys of| our you′th are | the da′ys of | our glo′ry.

❏ Know also some **Variations or Substitutions of metre & feet:**
- • We have already known there are **seven kinds of feet**. Out of them *'spondee'* and *'pyrrhic'* –fall to regular variations of disyllabic feet.
- • Besides them, there are some more variations. Of them only four we like to mention here. They are:
1) **Catalectic: (stopping short)** [consists of one accented syllable only. Generally used at the end of a disyllabic or trisyllabic foot]
   - ➢ 'Lea′rn to | la′-bour | a′nd to | wai′t.'
2) **Hypermetrical: (beyond meter)** [refers to a line which has one or two syllables at its end. It is presumed that these syllables (after an accented syllable) are in excel of what is required by the normal metrical pattern. These superfluous syllables are not

counted as a foot and indicated by the sign ([ ). They look like a pyrrhic, but not regarded as.]

> A thi ′ ng | of beau ′ - | ty i ′ s | a jo ′ y | for e ′ v- [er.
> There wa ′ s | an a ′ n- | cient sa ′ ge | phi-lo ′ s- [o-pher.

3) **Acephalous: (headless)** [consists of one accented syllable only, used at the beginning of a disyllabic metre, as opposed to catalectic, relating position.]

> Lau ′ gh- | ter ho ′ ld- | ing bo ′ th | his si ′ des.

4) **Anacrusis: (pushing back)** [consists of one unaccented syllable used at the beginning of a disyllabic or trisyllabic foot, as opposed to 'Acephalous' regarding accent. All the above including this one is presumed as an excess of what is required by the normal metrical pattern. This superfluous syllable is not counted as a foot, and is indicated by the sign ( ])]

> We] loo ′ k be- | fo ′ re and | a ′ f-ter
> In] de-fe ′ nce | of my | trea ′ -sure

Pause & Rhyme (Rime)

Pause: A Pause (from Greek 'pausis' meaning '**stop**') is a stop in the course of our reading during which the voice is given some rest. It is a characteristic of both prose and verse. In the case of verses, it may be affected by the demands of sense or metrical pattern. In verse, this pause actually represented by the **unaccented syllables** & different **punctuations** as usual we use in language (as, comma, semicolon, full-stop, exclamation or question mark, etc.); as,

o 'Pi ′ -per | pla ′ y! | Pi ′ -per | pla ′ y!
o 'The rai ′ n | bow co ′ me | and goe ′ s.'
o 'Hope spri ′ ngs | e-te ′ r- |nal in ′ | the hu ′ - |man brea ′ st.'

☐ The pause comes at the end of a poetic line is called the **'Final Metrical Pause'** or **'Final Pause'**, may represented by common punctuations, comma, semicolon, colon, hyphen, dash or full stop.
☐ A pause more or less in the middle of a line is known as **'Caesura'**, represented by two vertical lines [||].
o Honour and shame|| from no condition rise,
o Act well your part|| there all the honour lies. (Pope)

Rhyme (Rime): Similar sound of one or more words at the end of succeeding lines of a verse or poem, is known as 'Rhyme' (also spelt as 'Rime'); as,

○ Grow old along with *me*!
○ The best is yet to *be*!

Here, the word '**me**' is rhymed with '**be**'; and thus, that may be like — day, say; play, bay; ring, sing; puff, ruff; lies, eyes; cough, off; stead, bed; daughter, laughter, etc. it is to be noted that in rhyme it is the sound, not the spelling, that matters. According to Sterling, 'rhyme denotes the recurrence of similar sounds in the closing syllables of different <u>verses</u>' (**verses**: read, '<u>lines</u>'; however, verse also means 'a metrical line')

The Art of Scansion

❑ **Scansion:** Scansion (from Latin *'scandere'*, meaning 'to climb') is the art of identifying the metre of a poem or a part of it (i.e., of a line called a verse, or a series of lines called a stanza). <u>To scan a poem or an extract</u>, we have:
   a.   To divide each line into a number of feet,
      b.   count the number of feet in each line, and define as *monometer*, *dimeter*, *trimeter*, *tetrameter*, *pentameter*, etc.
   c.   <u>mark the accented syllable in each foot</u> with a slanted stroke ('), <u>and to name</u> the nature of such feet (*iamb*, *trochee*, *anapaest*, *dactyl* & *amphibrach*), and
   d.   mention the irregularities, if any (viz. spondee & pyrrhic etc.)

Note: <u>Scansion helps us to see the syllabic and rhythmic nature of the feet</u>, to know the metrical nature of a line or lines of a poem.
   But remember: In English, metres with a particular or singular foot are seldom found in their pure state; they are often mixed together. With Iamb there may have spondee or pyrrhic, and so on.

Scansion for Practice: **<u>Study the lines and scan them properly.</u>**

1. A-wa ' y! | A-wa ' y! | for I ' | will fly ' | to thee ',
   Not cha ' r- | io-te ' d | by Ba ' c- |chus an ' d | his pa ' rds,
   But o ' n | the vie ' w- | less wi ' ngs | of Po ' | esy ',
   Though the | du ' ll brai ' n | per-ple ' x- | es a ' nd | re-ta ' rds.
   ➢ prosodic name of the lines: Iambic pentameter is used with the following variations. The first and second feet of the last line are pyrrhic and spondee respectively.

2. As we ru ' sh, | as we ru ' sh, | in the trai ' n,
   The tree ' s | and the hou ' - | ses go whee ' l- | **ing ba ' ck,**

But the sta ′ r- | **ry hea ′ v-** | ens a-bo ′ ve | **the plai ′ n**
Come fly ′- | ing o ′ n | our tra ′ ck.
> prosodic name of the lines: Anapaestic trimeter and tetrameter are combined. There are iambic substitutions in the first and last feet of the second line, and the second and last feet of the third line. The last line is iambic.

3. A ′ rt is | lo ′ ng, and |Ti ′ me is | flee ′ ting,
A ′ nd our | hea ′ rts, though | stou ′ t and | **bra ′ ve,**
Sti ′ ll like | mu ′ f-fled | dru ′ ms, are | bea ′ t-ing
Fu ′ ne- | ral ma ′ rch- |es to ′ |the gra ′ ve.
> prosodic name of the lines: Trochaic tetrameter is used here. The last feet of the second line is catalectic.

4. A-lo ′ ne |a-lo ′ ne, | **a ′ ll, a ′ ll** | a-lo ′ ne,
A-lo ′ ne |on a wi ′ de | **wi ′ de sea′** !
And ne ′ v-|er a sai ′ nt | took pi ′ t- | y o ′ n
My sou ′ l | in a ′ - | go-ny ′.
> prosodic name of the lines: Iambic tetrameter and trimeter are used alternatively. There is anapestic substitution in the second foot each of the second and third lines. The third foot each of the first and second lines are spondee.

Verse Forms & Some Literary Terms

1. **Blank Verse:** A *verse form without Rime* (rhyme), generally *written in iambic pentameter*; the following extract is from Thomas Heywood's:
> Beggary, shame, death, scandal, and **reproach,**
> For you I'll hazard all: why, what care **I**?
> For you I'll live, and in your love I'll die.

2. **Free Verse:** A verse form that lacks both rhythm and rhyme (no rhythm i.e., 'no regular stress pattern) and has irregular line-lengths. It is said, modern poets are very much fond of this type of verse. As it ignores the rules of Prosody, Robert Frost remarks: 'Writing free-verse is like playing tennis with the net down.' See an example of free-verse:
> Yes, she also will turn middle-aged,
> And the glow of youth that she spread about us
> As she brought us our muffins

> Will be spread about us no longer.
> She also will turn middle-aged.   (Ezra Pound)

3. **Couplet:** It consists of two successive lines of verse rhyming together, especially in the same metre, e.g.

> The grave's a fine and private place,
> But none, I think, do there embrace.   (Marvell)

4. **Heroic Couplet:** Heroic couplet also consists of two successive lines, which is written in iambic pentameter. It is so called because of its frequent use in epic poetry. An example follows:

> Laugh where we must, be candid where we can;
> But vindicate the ways of God to man.   (Pope)

5. **Triplet:** It consists of a group of three successive lines having same rhyme, irrespective of the number of feet in each line, e.g.,

> Who e'er she be,
> That not impossible she
> That shall command my heart and me.   (Crashaw)

6. **Tercet:** A tercet is also of three lines, but has no similar rhyme like triplet, mainly used in *sestet* or in the *Terza Rima stanza.* The first line rhymes with third and second with first line of next Tercet and thus go on. *Haiku* is its Japanese variation. An example of Tercet:

a	Make me thy lyre, even as the forest is:
b	What if my leaves are falling like its own!
a	The tumult of thy mighty harmonies
b	Will take from both a deep, autumnal tone
c	Sweet though in sadness. Be thou spirit fierce
b	My spirit! Be thou me, impetuous one! (Shelley)

7. **Quatrain:** It is a verse of four lines having various rhyme schemes. It is the commonest stanza form in English. The following quatrain follows the rhyme of –a b a b:

a	We lay beneath a spreading oak,
b	Beside a mossy seat;
a	And from the turf a fountain broke
b	And gurgled at our feet. (Wordsworth)

8. **Quintain:** This verse form consists of five lines rhyming in various combinations. It is also known as *Quintet.*

A	Go, lovely Rose!
B	Tell her that wastes her time and me,

a   That now she knows,
b   When I resemble her to thee,
b   How sweet and fair she seems to be. (Waller)

9. **Sextain:** It is also called *sestet*. It consists of six lines having various rhyme schemes. One scheme is as the following:

a   Leave to the nightingale her shady wood;
b   A privacy of glorious light is thine,
a   When thou dost pour upon the world a flood
b   Of harmony, with instinct more divine;
c   Type of the wise, who soar, but never roam—
c   True to the kindred points of Heaven and Home!

(Wordsworth)

10. **Septet:** It consists of seven lines having various rhyme schemes. One such form is **Rhyme Royal** (named after King James I of Scotland) written in iambic pentameter with rhyme scheme—a b a b b c c :

a   Now stole upon the time the dead of night,
b   When heavy sleep have clos'd up mortal eyes:
a   No comfortable star did lend his light;
b   No noise but owl's and wolves' death boding cries;
b   Now serves the season that they may surprise
c   The silly lamb; pure thoughts are dead and still,
c   While lust and murder wake to stain and kill.

(Shakespeare)

11. **Octet:** It consists of eight lines having various rhyme schemes. One such form is **Ottava Rima,** written in iambic pentameter. First six lines rhyme alternatively while the last two form a couplet.

A   His suite consisted of three servants and
b   A tutor, the licentiate Pedrillo,
a   Who several languages did understand,
b   But now lay sick and speechless in his pillow,
a   And rocking in his hammock, long'd for land,
b   His headache being increased by every billow;
c   And the waves oozing through the port-hole made
c   His berth a little damp, and him afraid. (Byron)

12. **Nonet:** It consists of nine lines having various combination of rhymes. One such form is the **Spenserian Stanza** (named after Edmund Spenser, its inventor), written in eight iambic pentameter lines followed by an **Alexandrine** (i.e., an iambic hexameter). Such an example is the following:

a   Roll on, thou deep and dark-blue Ocean, roll,

b	Ten thousand fleets sweep over thee in vain:
a	Man marks the earth with ruin; his control
b	Stops with the shore; upon the watery main
b	The wrecks are all thy deed; nor doth remain
c	A shadow of man's ravage save his own,
b	When for a moment like a drop of rain
c	He sinks into thy depths with bubbling groan,
c	Without a grave, unknelled, unconfined, and unknown.

(Byron)

13. **Sonnet:** It come from Latin word **'*sonus*'**, meaning **'*sound*'**. It is a poem in which one thought is developed in a single stanza of fourteen lines in pentameter verse form, usually divided into two patterns—the **Italian** (or Regular or Petrarchan) and the **English** (or Elizabethan or Shakespearean). The **Petrarchan sonnet** is divided by a pause into **octave** and **sestet. The octave** consists of two quatrains having the following rhyme scheme: **ab ba, ab ba. The sestet consists of two tercets usually having the following rhyme scheme: cdc, dcd,** or **cde, cde.**

However, the **Shakespearean Sonnet** consists of three quatrains **(ab ab, cd cd, ef ef)** and a concluding couplet **(g g)**. And it has variance too, like the **Spenserian Sonnet (ab ab, bc bc, cd cd)** and a concluding couplet **(e e)**.

<u>The following is the example of a Petrarchan sonnet:</u>

a	To one who has been long in city pent
b	'Tis very sweet to look into the fair
b	And open face of heavens, --to breathe a prayer
a	Full in the smile of the blue firmament.
a	Who is more happy, when, with heart's content,
b	Fatigued he sinks into some pleasant lair
b	Of wavy grass, and reads a debonair
a	And gentle tale of love and languishment?
c	Returning home at evening with an air
d	Catching the notes of Philomel, --an eye
c	Watching the sailing cloudlet's bright career
d	He mourns that day so soon has glided by,
c	E'en like the passage of an angel's tear
d	That falls through the clear ether silently. (Keats)

❑ **Other Verse forms**

14. **Lyric:** The lyric originally meant a poem to be sung to the accompaniment of a lyre which flourished in the Middle Ages in France and Italy. In England, Chaucer is the greatest pioneer of this new kind of poetry. However later, the accompaniment of a lyre was dropped and the musical quality was retained by word-music or sheer verbal melody. The artistic arrangement of vowels and consonants make a lyric musical. Odes, ballads, sonnet —are some of its popular forms.

15. **Carols:** One of the earliest lyric forms, belong to the song tradition. It, usually, consists of a quatrain and a couplet serving as a refrain.

16. **The Ballad:** A lyrical folk song, mainly sung by minstrels and folk-dancers. In other words, it is a simple short story in verse, dealing with common events and actions. The theme may be love, war, adventure, harvesting, and so on. Sometimes the themes are fierce or tragic. Coleridge's "The Rime of the Ancient Mariner" is such an example.

17. **The Ode:** The word 'ode' in Greek, its origin, means a song. Ode has two forms—the Pindaric (named after Pinder, a Greek poet) and Horatian Ode (named after Horace, the Roman poet). English odes follow the classical Greek tradition, mainly, in subject matter, treatment and style and amalgamating with it their new theme, i.e., included their mystic experiences. The romantic poets like Shelley, Keats took the ode to lofty heights, pouring their thoughts and sentiments in 'unpremeditated art' into it. Keats' *'Ode to Grecian Urn', 'Ode to Nightingale', 'Ode to Autumn'* are some finest examples.

18. **The Elegy:** The elegy has its roots in ancient Greece. The term was at one time applied to a wide range of subjects both grave and gay, covering war songs, love poems, political verses, lamentations for the dead and so on. However, presently, it only applies to poems, lamenting the dead of a friend, near ones or an eminent person. *Shelley's 'Adonais', Milton's 'Lycidas', Arnold' 'Thyrsis' are* the examples of pastoral elegies.

About Mr. Peter

Mr. Peter is a penname of the writer, an Indian and a teacher in West Bengal. Most of his academic works are the products of his professional career what he held over twenty years and continuing… Mr. Peter loves to publish his books in the self-publishing platforms, like Amazon (worldwide) and notionpress.com (India). For this, Peter heartily pays his gratitude to Amazon, notionpress.com and for marketing to Flipkart, Amazon & different social media. Presently, Mr. Peter's books are available in 3 formats—eBook, Paperback & Hardcover. Mr. Peter's books which are published at Notion Press Pvt. Ltd., Chennai, are available to buy on **notionpress.com, Flipkart**, **Amazon**.in

Discounts, promotions, etc. are available in all platforms. However, if one seeks special offers for marketing or wants to give bulk order, s/he may visit only to **notionpress.com** (type **Mr. Peter** in the search box, and use following **Coupon Codes:** (If not work, for the current status, one may contact by https://www.facebook.com/profile.php?id=100081822070172 or (5) Books Campaigns, Free Coupons, Learning English Grammar & Composition | Facebook

notionpress.com/en/coupon_manager

books ▾ Author Dashboard My Shelf

Mr. Peter

Campaign Name	Book Name	Coupon Type	Discount %	Discounted Price	Used Count	Report	Actions
bulk01	Peter's 'English Grammar'	Bulk-Use	30	~~₹ 1201~~ ₹ 841	0/100	Download	Delete
unique01	Peter's 'English Grammar'	Multi-Use	23	~~₹ 1201~~ ₹ 925	0/100	Download	Delete
bulk00	A Book of Advanced Writing Skill, the Complete Version (incl Part-1, 2 & 3)	Bulk-Use	23	~~₹ 780~~ ₹ 601	1/100	Download	Delete
unique00	A Book of Advanced Writing Skill, the Complete Version (incl Part-1, 2 & 3)	Multi-Use	15	~~₹ 780~~ ₹ 663	0/100	Download	Delete
DEAL11	Development of Writing Skill, Part-3	Bulk-Use	24	~~₹ 365~~ ₹ 278	0/10	Download	Delete
PUJADEAL10	Development of Writing Skill, Part-3	Multi-Use	18	~~₹ 365~~ ₹ 300	0/10	Download	Delete
DEAL10	Development of Writing Skill, Part-2	Bulk-Use	24	~~₹ 365~~ ₹ 278	1/10	Download	Delete
PUJADEAL9	Development of Writing Skill, Part-2	Multi-Use	18	~~₹ 365~~ ₹ 300	0/10	Download	Delete
PujaDeal8	Steps to Composition (Development of Writing Skill, from Primary to Secondary Level)	Multi-Use	20	~~₹ 300~~ ₹ 240	1/10	Download	Delete
PujaDeal7	Rhetoric & Prosody	Multi-Use	20	~~₹ 240~~ ₹ 192	0/10	Download	Delete
PujaDeal6	Question Bank of English Grammar & Composition	Multi-Use	20	~~₹ 559~~ ₹ 448	0/10	Download	Delete
PujaDeal5	Study of Subject-Verb Agreement, Narration Change, Use of Punctuation; including Analysis, Synthesis & Split-up	Multi-Use	20	~~₹ 301~~ ₹ 241	0/10	Download	Delete
PujaDeal4	Detail Study of Phrases, Clauses & Sentences, including Idioms & Phrasal Verbs	Multi-Use	20	~~₹ 290~~ ₹ 232	0/10	Download	Delete
PujaDeal3	Study of Adverbs, Prepositions, Conjunctions & Interjections	Multi-Use	20	~~₹ 260~~ ₹ 208	0/10	Download	Delete